Gorgeous Cross-Stitch

Editor: Bobbe Needham
Art Director: Kathy Holmes
Production: Elaine Thompson
English Translation: Networks, Inc.
Editorial Assistance: Stephanie Johnston and Ethan Skemp

**Library of Congress Cataloging-in-Publication Data
Available**

A Sterling/Lark Book

Produced by Altamont Press, Inc.
   50 College St., Asheville, NC 28801

Published in 1995 by Sterling Publishing Co., Inc.
   387 Park Ave. S., New York, NY 10016

Pages 65–67: Photos and original instructions © Libelle
Special/Uitgeverij Spaarnestad, Haarlem, Holland

Other project photos and original instructions ©
Ariadne/Spaarnestad, Utrecht, Holland

English translation © 1995, Altamont Press

Distributed in Canada by Sterling Publishing,
   c/o Canadian Manda Group, One Atlantic Avenue, Suite 105,
   Toronto, Ontario M6K 3E7

Distributed in the United Kingdom by Cassell PLC, Villiers House,
   41/47 Strand, London WC2N 5JE, England

Distributed in Australia by Capricorn Link (Australia) Pty Ltd.
   P.O. Box 6651, Baulkham Hills, Business Centre, NSW 2153, Australia

Printed in Hong Kong

ISBN 0-8069-0974-9

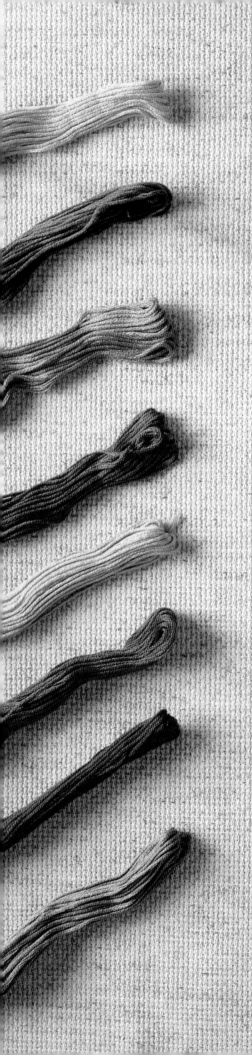

Contents

Introduction

All through my growing-up years, a cross-stitched sampler hung on the wall of my parents' bedroom, next to the oval mirror over my mother's dresser. The wallpaper behind it changed from blue to cream to lilies of the valley, but the sampler stayed, its little house and simple sentiment among the fixed points of my childhood. Great-grandmother Smith made it when she was a little girl in College Corner, Ohio. "Home is where the heart is," she had stitched in angular black letters, "love is where the home is." I believed it.

There is still something about work done by hand that carries its own truth for me. When I see a hand-turned chair, an egg-gathering basket, a bright afghan, a cross-stitched picture, for just a moment I imagine the woodworker, the basket weaver, the knitter, the needleworker bent over their work. I glimpse calloused hands, a rounded back, a quiet smile, a needle glinting in firelight. How could each piece not absorb something of its maker?

For me, cross-stitch has always had a particular simplicity and elegance. For century upon century, women and men have created exquisite designs with the most basic of figures, the x. Stitching with bright strands of silk or cotton thread on linen and canvas stretched on simple hoops or mahogany frames, they have made works of art of blouses and bedspreads, decorated layettes and trousseaus, filled hope chests, and beautified curtains in Greek cottages, silk hangings in China, West African robes, and rugs for Queen Victoria. It is a timeless art.

But it is the sense of personal history that cross-stitch conveys, I believe, that gives it special value. As the sampler of my childhood carried the aura of my great-grandmother, each project in this book brings with it the opportunity to create not only beauty but—for someone, sometime—a memory.

INSTRUCTIONS FOR THIS PROJECT APPEAR ON PAGE 83.

Cross-Stitch Basics

You need to follow only one basic guideline to create a beautiful piece of cross-stitch: work all the upper crossing stitches in the same direction—say, from the lower left to the upper right of the x. If you cross the stitches in different directions, the light will reflect differently off them in the finished work and make them look uneven. The good news is that this phenomenon works in your favor if you want to emphasize a part of the design: just switch the direction of your upper stitches in that area.

Most cross-stitchers work back and forth across a pattern in rows, slanting all the lower threads the same way as they travel in one direction and the upper threads the other way as they journey back across the row, as shown here.

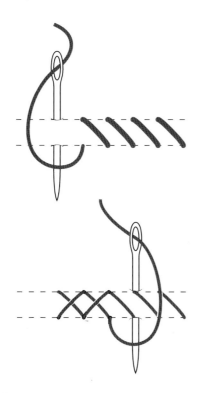

CROSS-STITCHING A STRAIGHT ROW

For diagonal rows of stitches, scattered individual stitches, or single stitches of one color, the easiest method is to complete one stitch at a time.

Deciding on Fabrics

All cross-stitch patterns require you to count the threads of your fabric, and you make each cross over an intersection of those threads. This means, first, that the threads need to be distinct enough for you to count them. Second, the ideal fabric is an even-weave, with the same number of warp and weft threads per inch (2.5 cm). On any other fabric, the cross-stitches will be uneven.

Any even-weave fabric will work, but a fabric that a veteran cross-stitcher finds challenging and satisfying might discourage a beginner. The closer the weave—that is, the more threads to the inch—the more difficult and exacting the needlework. Each project in this book tells you in a paragraph on materials what fabric appears in the pictured example, including its thread count.

Popular and easy-to-find fabrics include linen, Aida, Hardanger, and canvas. Probably the most expensive of these, linen is both beautiful and durable and comes in weaves from coarse to fine. Aida cloth, a cotton blend, has between eight and eighteen threads per inch. Another cotton blend, Hardanger cloth, with twenty-two threads to the inch, resists fraying and thus proves especially useful when designs require you to cut sections out.

Tip

Four things to know about Aida cloth:

• Unless the instructions suggest it, don't launder Aida cloth before you embroider your project.

• To avoid fraying, zigzag machine stitch twice around the edges or press under 1/4 inch (1 cm) along the raw edges and whipstitch or machine stitch in place. (Some projects include other suggestions for raw edges.)

• The cloth draws together in areas with a heavy concentration of cross-stitching.

• The fabric shrinks from 1/2 to 3/4 inches (1.5 to 2 cm) when you wash the finished piece with soap and water, but this tightening gives the final product a trim, neat look.

Using the Charts

A chart, or graph, of the embroidered motif appears with each project in the book. The key to each chart lists a different symbol for each color of embroidery floss you will use for the project. On the chart for the butterfly shown here, for instance, the dots stand for blue and the z's for turquoise.

On the chart, each square with a symbol in it represents one cross-stitch on your fabric. For the butterfly, on the bottom row you make one blue stitch; on the second row, another blue stitch above it and one to the right; on the third row, working from left to right, two blue stitches, then two turquoise stitches, and so on.

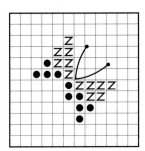

●	blue
z	turquoise

SIMPLE CHART

To center the design you intend to embroider on your fabric, fold the fabric end to end, then side to side to locate the center. Mark both centerlines with tailor's chalk, straight pins, or basting thread. Your goal is to match the center of the chart to the center of the fabric, so the embroidery doesn't run off one side of the piece.

The directions for many projects in this book suggest where to begin stitching the design. To keep your place on the chart, you might move a small ruler or index card down the rows as you work or pencil through each row as you complete it.

Selecting Needles and Floss

Cross-stitchers use tapestry needles, which hold multiple strands of floss and push the fabric fibers apart without splitting threads or previous stitches. (Avoid crewel needles, designed to pierce fabric threads.) The more coarse the fabric weave, the larger the needle needs to be. A packet of assorted sizes (say, 20 to 24) will work for most fabrics. The higher the number, the smaller the needle.

The six-strand cotton embroidery floss used in cross-stitching comes in a rainbow of colors. Each skein runs approximately nine yards (8.2 m). For each project in this book, the key to the chart suggests floss colors and for each color supplies the corresponding product number for two widely available brands of floss. (You may of course substitute another brand—or rewrite the color key altogether.)

Especially when your project calls for many colors of floss, you may yearn for a way to organize all those skeins. Craft or fabric shops offer a variety of organizers, but you can easily make one.

Punch holes along the sides of a stiff card or piece of cardboard. Then cut one skein of the floss called for in your project to lengths of about a yard (.9 m) each. Hold one end of the lengths together and thread through a hole in the cardboard, as shown here. Label each skein with its symbol on the key to the project chart, its brand, and its shade number.

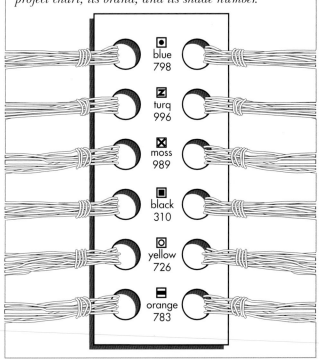

Thinking about Embroidery Hoops

Using an embroidery hoop to hold the fabric taut as you work is a question of personal preference. Some cross-stitchers find that hoops slow them down or distort their stitches. Others feel that hoops help keep the stitching even. Whether or not you use a hoop, ironing the finished embroidery takes care of any fabric creases or unevenness of tension in the stitches.

A hoop requires you to sew with the stab-stitch method—that is, straight down through the fabric, then straight up, in two separate motions. Without a hoop, you have the option of slipping the needle from hole to hole in a down-up-down pattern, which for many stitchers moves faster.

The hoop of choice is a two-ring wood or plastic frame that you can adjust with a screw on the outer ring.

Working Cross-Stitch

A short length of floss works best for cross-stitching—about fourteen to twenty-four inches (36 to 62 cm). Unlike many kinds of sewing, in cross-stitch you don't knot your thread. As you pull the first stitch of your project or of a new area through the fabric, leave a one-inch (2.5 cm) tail of floss dangling free at the back, then catch this tail under the next few stitches.

Once you have several rows worked, start a new strand by running your needle under a few already worked stitches on the back of the design, then come up on the right side to begin stitching. At the end of a color or strand, run the last inch or so of floss under four or five stitches on the back of the work and snip off the excess.

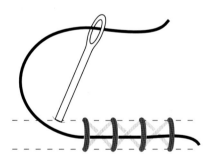

CATCHING THE FLOSS TAIL

Plan ahead with colors. For instance, you may stitch a spring green in a flower petal and see that it will appear later in the stem. Rather than starting and stopping your strand like a new driver at every intersection, after completing the petal carry the long remaining strand to an out-of-the-way spot on the fabric, pull it through, and take the needle off, as shown here in the drawing of the vase. When you reach the stem, pull the dangling strand through to the back of the work, rethread it, and travel on the wrong side to the stem, weaving through your newly embroidered stitches.

PLANNING AHEAD WITH COLORS

Adapting Other Fabrics

If you have cross-stitch projects in mind that you don't want to work on even-weave fabric, you have plenty of alternatives: adding decorative bands or scraps of even-weave, stitching on gingham, creating a canvas grid, or taking advantage of premade items.

Bands and borders. You can find strips of even-weave fabric an inch or two wide (2.5 to 5 cm) at craft or fabric shops. For borders on bath and bed linens, shirts and skirts, or children's clothing, pick the motif you like, cross-stitch the strips, then sew them on—or sew the band on first and stitch through both fabrics. Examples of the technique in the book include the train sheet, jungle towel, and bear blanket.

Fabric scraps. You can sew any size piece of even-weave fabric to anything you can get a needle through—a canvas backpack or fanny pack, for example, or as a pocket on a shirt or apron. You might tack the fabric to the item and cross-stitch your design through both thicknesses. Then fray and trim the edges of the even-weave close to the design. Depending on the wear the finished item will undergo, another option involves cross-stitching on the even-weave, turning the excess under, and whipstitching or machine stitching the embroidered piece in place. In the book, the kid badges and the backpack call for this technique.

Checked gingham. Any checked fabric offers you a ready-made cross-stitch grid. Working the stitches over the colored squares means you don't need to count threads. The size of the checks determines stitch size.

Needlepoint canvas. To decorate fabric with an uneven weave, you can create a temporary cross-stitch grid on needlepoint canvas that you will remove when your project is complete. Baste a fine, single-weave canvas (not one with an interlocking mesh) to the piece where you want your design to be. With the canvas as your grid, cross-stitch through it and the fabric.

When you have completed your motif, remove the basting and trim the canvas close to the embroidery, taking care not to snip your cross-stitching. Then you can remove the grid, first drawing out all the strands of canvas that run in one direction, then all the strands that run the other way.

Tip

You can give a piece of white or ivory linen an antique look by soaking the washed material in strong, cold tea for about ten minutes, stirring occasionally. Allow the piece to drip dry, and iron before cross-stitching. Aging works just as well for an already embroidered piece, as long as the thread is color fast.

Ready-made items. Many craft and fabric stores carry items that incorporate bands or sections of cross-stitch fabric—terry towels, bibs and infant wear, glasses cases, tote bags, place mats, afghans, bread cloths.

Changing Sizes

Vary the finished size of a design by making your cross-stitches larger or smaller—that is, by crossing more or fewer threads than the instructions call for.

When you want to use a fabric different from that called for in project instructions, or when you design your own work, plan your stitch size based on the effect you want. On a fabric with fewer (thus, fatter) threads per inch, crossing two threads for each stitch gives you good-sized stitches. Crossing two threads on a fine-woven fabric that has more threads per inch results in tiny, fine stitches.

Tip

The more threads of fabric you cross with one stitch, the less solid the mass of color that will result, because more fabric will show behind the stitches. The more strands of floss you use, the thicker and bolder the stitch. Stitches usually look best when they fill the holes of the fabric without losing the clarity of the cross.

ITEMS YOU CAN BUY THAT INCORPORATE CROSS-STITCH FABRIC INCLUDE, CLOCKWISE FROM LEFT: TOTE BAG, INFANT TOWEL, BIB AND INFANT CUP, POTHOLDER, CHRISTMAS STOCKING, AND HAND TOWEL.

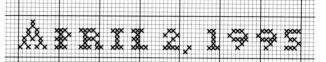

2. Count the number of spaces allowed between each letter in a word (here, 2), each number in a date (2), and each complete word or date (4).

3. If you want to include commas, periods, or hyphens, count the spaces between a word or date and a mark of punctuation (here, 2).

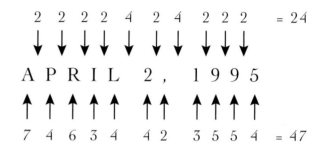

4. To make your own chart on graph paper, first mark the beginning and end points of the spaces allowed on a line of your project. In this example, we have eighty-one spaces to work with. Divide by two to find the center point on the chart (in this case, forty-one). Add up the spaces between letters and words (here, they total twenty-four). Add this figure to the total of the letter and number spaces (here, forty-seven). Here the total of the spaces plus the letters and numbers is seventy-one. We have a fit, with five squares of space left on each side (81-71=10).

You can design your own letters and numbers or adapt the style from any project. You may want to work with various sizes and styles to find what best fits your spacing and the style of your piece. If you find you have extra space, you can repeat symbols from elsewhere in the piece. To shrink lines you can abbreviate words, substitute initials for names, and so on.

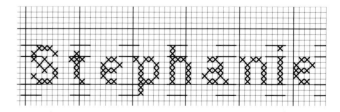

BASTING GUIDELINES

To avoid frustration, give yourself guidelines for names, dates, and borders, as shown in the name **Stephanie** here: frame tricky sections of your motif

Choosing Colors

Taste, personal preference, decor, mood, the weather—anything you choose can govern the colors of your cross-stitch project. Each project chart in this book comes with a color key that reflects the floss colors used in the pictured projects, but feel free to design your own palette. A color tip: When choosing floss, lay it over the fabric you will use under natural light.

Tip

To learn if a particular color of floss will bleed, wash the skein in plenty of lukewarm water. If it bleeds, rinse with cold water until the water runs clear. Don't wring the floss, but fold it in a towel to press out the moisture, then let it dry.

Changing Letters and Numbers

You will nearly always want to substitute other names and dates for the ones pictured on the samplers in this book (except perhaps for the historic samplers). Let's say you want one line of your sampler to read "April 2, 1995," as shown here. On the original project chart:

1. Count across to find the cross-stitches allowed on each line (in this case, 81).

by basting straight lines with bright-colored, single strands of floss. When you finish cross-stitching that area, remove the basting.

Other Stitches

Most projects in the book suggest that you embroider around your finished cross-stitch with an outline stitch; the projects also call for a smattering of other common embroidery stitches.

Chain stitch. Used for both filling and outlining, the stitch runs along a marked or imaginary line. Bring the needle to the right side of your work along the line and hold the thread down with your thumb. Take the needle back through the fabric very close to the same spot and bring its point up a short distance along the line, with the thread looped under the tip of the needle. Pull the thread through.

Daisy stitch. In the book this single chain stitch occurs most often for flower petals. Follow the chain stitch steps, but bring your needle out for succeeding stitches in a flower shape (or whatever the project chart calls for) rather than in a chain.

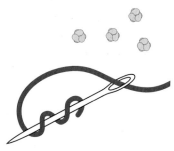

French knot. Often used in the book for eyes or flower centers, French knots add texture to your work. Working on the right side of your piece, wrap the thread twice around the point of your needle, pull it tight, and insert the needle next to where it came out. Hold the thread taut to form a clean knot. To make a larger knot, wrap the thread more times around the needle.

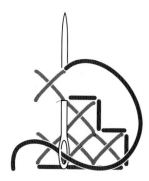

Outline stitch. Also called the back stitch, this basic stitch works for any outlining called for in the book. On the right side of your work, bring the needle up to the right of the figure you want to outline, take a small stitch backward, and bring the needle up again in front of the first stitch, a stitch-length away. As you work along the line, insert your needle each time at the end of the previous stitch.

Running stitch. In this simplest of stitches, bring the needle to the right side of your work and stitch from right to left, crossing the same number of threads with each stitch.

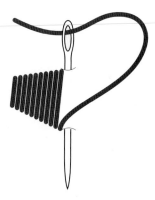

Satin stitch. This stitch often occurs in projects for filling in flower centers, mouths, and other areas that need solid color. The idea is to completely cover the fabric with flat, even stitches. On the right side of your work, bring the needle up at the lower edge of the area you want to cover and insert the needle directly across the area from that entry point. Make each stitch right beside the previous one.

Slip stitch. This basic sewing stitch makes an almost invisible hem, a join between two folded edges of fabric, or a join between a folded edge and a flat piece of fabric. Pull the thread just enough for a secure join; too much tension will wrinkle the fabric.

Stem stitch. A popular outline stitch, stem stitches appear in the projects for working the stems of flowers and leaves and for animals' mouths. Bring the needle up to the right side of your work along a line, insert it just to the right of the line, and bring it back up half a stitch-length back. As you work along the line, bring your needle up each time at the end of the previous stitch for a continuous, braided look.

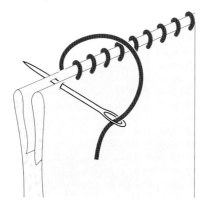

Whipstitch. Used instead of a slip stitch for a stronger join, whipstitch is worked from right to left, taking up a small amount of fabric from each folded edge. Pull the thread taut for a neat join.

Making Mitered Corners

Anytime you fold corners under to mat a sampler or hem them for a tablecloth, a blanket, or curtains, mitering is an easy technique that makes the corners lie neat and flat.

1. Fold or iron 1/4 inch (1 cm) of fabric to the wrong side to make an inner hem.

2. Fold again to make the outer hem and iron or press hard to hold the crease. Open the outer hem.

3. Fold a corner to the wrong side and iron. Leaving a 1/4 inch (1 cm) seam allowance, trim the corner.

4. Fold both outer hems in along the crease and pin. The edges will meet to form a diagonal seam at the corner. Slip stitch the seam closed.

Tip

Mistakes don't have to be forever. As you unpick your stitches back to where things went wrong, put as little strain as possible on the fabric to avoid pulling its threads out of line or enlarging holes. Cut the thread you are picking out often, so that you only have to pull out short strands. Before you resew, you might even go over the unpicked area with sticky tape to remove every trace of thread.

Washing and Pressing

If your finished project needs washing, launder washable fabrics and floss like any other delicate items: slosh gently in lukewarm water and mild soap, then rinse. Depending on the fabric and project, either (1) roll it in a towel to blot up excess moisture, then hang or lay flat to dry, or (2) machine dry and remove the item from the dryer while it is still slightly damp.

To iron out wrinkles and unevenness, cover your ironing board with a towel, then a soft cloth—ironing on a towel helps push the stitches out from the fabric, rather than flattening them down. Place your work face down on the cloth and cover it with another soft cloth, dampened if your piece is dry. Press lightly with a fairly hot iron. Then lay the embroidery flat until it dries completely.

Cottage Garden Sampler

*Even Agatha Christie couldn't have resisted the charming
British-teatime mood of this sampler. Possible titles:
"Murder on the Cross-Stitch Express," "Mystery in My Cottage
Garden." Doesn't the gingham mat enhance the
English-village feel? A different mat, a different mood.*

Finished Measurements
18-3/4 x 21-1/2 in. (48 x 55 cm)
Embroidery Measurements
13 x 15 in. (33.5 x 38.5 cm)

Materials

25-1/4 x 29-1/4 in. (65 x 75 cm) of white linen with 30 threads per inch (2.5 cm) and DMC or Anchor embroidery floss as indicated on the key to the chart plus black #310 or #403, dark grape #333 or #119, salmon #352 or #9, light navy #797 or #132, dark blush #962 or #75, and medium pink #3716 or #25. For the mat pictured: a piece of checked fabric 19-1/2 x 21-1/2 in. (50 x 55 cm), book-binding glue, a piece of stiff cardboard 19-1/4 x 21-1/2 in. (49.5 x 55 cm), and a craft knife.

Directions

Begin embroidering with the lower right corner of the pattern, placing the corner square of the pattern 6-1/4 in. (16 cm) from the edge of the linen. Work all stitches with two strands of floss over two threads of linen. Work the flowers in the border with daisy stitches and French knots. Fill in the daisy stitches with satin stitch.

Work in outline stitch in and around the house in dark charcoal and along the azure doorpost and windowpane in azure; in and around the grape border flowers at the upper left and at the lower center in medium grape; in and around the lower right border flowers in navy; in and around the yellow border flowers at upper left with medium light salmon; in and around the gray-and-white border flowers at upper right with medium light avocado. Outline stitch around the centers of the pink flowers in the lower right border and around the doorknob in black #310 or #403. On all other outline stitches work around figures in a matching or slightly darker shade.

For the garden flowers to the left of the house, work the daisy stitch with white and embroider the hearts with French knots in light orange. For the garden

flowers to the right, work the daisy stitch with grape and embroider the hearts with French knots in peach. Embroider the plums with medium pink #3716 or #25 and the lower garden flowers in medium light jonquil.

To frame the finished sampler as shown, cut a piece from the center of the cardboard 14-1/4 x 16-1/2 in. (36.5 x 42 cm). Trim and fit the covering fabric to the cardboard, leaving a half inch (1.5 cm) at the edges. Turn the edges under and glue. Mat and frame the sampler.

Key to Chart

		DMC	Anchor
·	= white	white	2
◨	= jade	320	215
◤	= grape	340	118
�	= light grape	341	117
‖	= medium light jade	368	214
◹	= very light lime	369	1043
▼	= dark charcoal	413	401
◸	= tan	437	362
X	= medium fog	452	232
◳	= light fog	453	231
◰	= medium pine	502	877
⦂	= light pine	503	875
▭	= light jade	504	213
⊞	= azure	518	1039
⊠	= green	522	860
◹	= light gray green	524	858
Z	= medium light pewter	647	1040
∴	= very light ecru	712	926
◖	= medium light jonquil	726	295
⦂⦂	= light sand	739	885
✳	= light orange	743	302
V	= peach	745	300
∩	= light cocoa	754	1012
◜	= medium light coral	760	1022
⋉	= light coral	761	1021
◫	= silver	762	234

		DMC	Anchor
⊔	= very light loden green	772	259
◢	= medium blue	798	142
⊙	= medium cobalt	809	130
⌐	= light pink	818	23
⦂·	= very light pink	819	271
◤	= dark fawn	840	379
◪	= medium fawn	841	378
⊤	= medium ecru	842	388
○	= light blush	963	73
◺	= medium light green	987	244
◹	= light green	988	243
+	= khaki	3012	843
◿	= light khaki	3013	842
⊔	= light silver	3024	397
◺	= linen	3033	391
◺	= very light jonquil	3078	292
◼	= med. dark avocado	3345	268
◿	= med. light avocado	3347	266
⦂⦂	= light loden green	3364	260
◣	= light magenta	3688	60
◖	= light carmine	3689	48
⦂⦂	= very light coral	3713	1020
◼	= medium maroon	3731	77
◢	= dark blush	3733	75
◝	= light blueberry	3747	120
◥	= dark cocoa	3772	1007

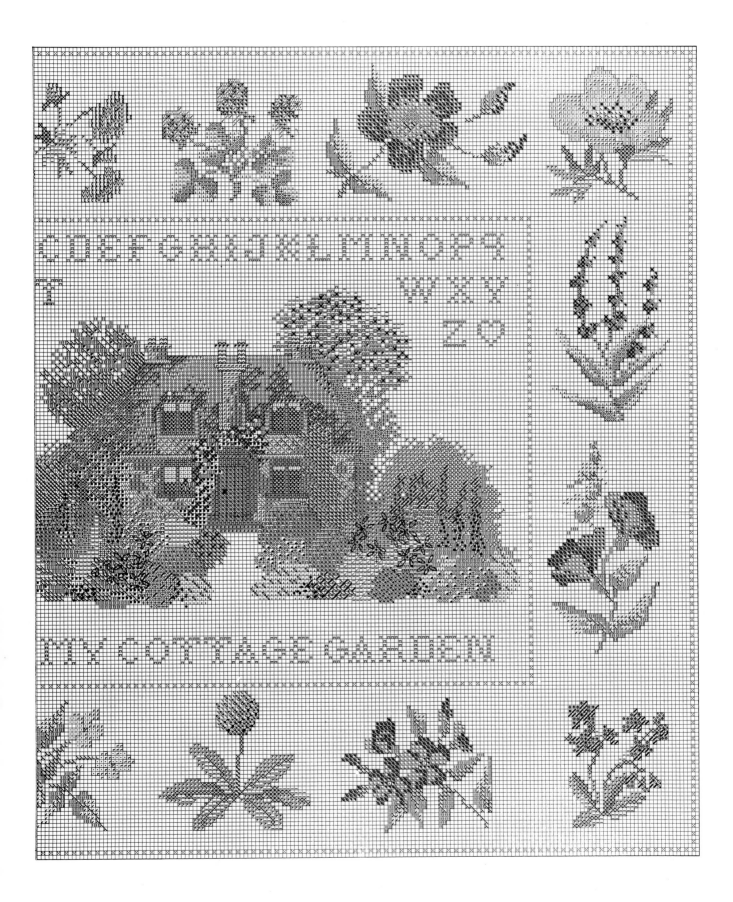

Cottage Garden Table Linens

Accessorize, accessorize—tablecloth and napkins to match your sampler, a couch to match your tablecloth…where will it all end?

A plaid lawn? A gingham dog?

Tablecloth Finished Measurements
62 x 77 (157 x 196 cm)

Napkin Finished Measurements
14 x 14 in. (36 x 36 cm)

Materials

For cloth and four napkins, 2-1/3 yd. (2.1 m) of ecru linen 54-1/2 in. (140 cm) wide with 36 threads per inch (2.5 cm); 2-1/2 yd. (2.3 m) of light-blue-and-ecru-checked fabric 45 in. (115 cm) wide; DMC or Anchor embroidery floss as indicated on the key to the chart for the sampler.

Directions
Tablecloth

Cut a piece of linen 53 x 68 in. (135 x 174 cm) for the main part of the cloth. For the checked borders, cut two strips 11 x 75 in. (28 x 193 cm) and two strips 11 x 59-1/2 in. (28 x 153 cm).

Embroider the flowers along the edges of the tablecloth according to the chart for the sampler. Work each cross-stitch using two strands of floss over three threads of linen. Place the flowers between 1-1/4 and 2-1/4 in. (3.5 and 6 cm) from the edge. Rotate the flowers at the corners a quarter turn so that their stems points to the corners.

Begin in one corner with the first flower and follow the chart. Embroider the second flower 8-1/2 in. (22 cm) from the side edge. Continue embroidering around the edges, placing the flowers about 5 in. (13 cm) apart, measured from center to center. Outline stitch over completed cross-stitch as for the sampler.

For the border, fold each of the checked strips in half lengthwise and trim off the corners away from the fold at a 45-degree angle. Flatten the pieces back out. Place a long piece and a short piece right sides together so that the pointed ends match up. Sew the ends together, making a 1/4 in. (1 cm) seam. Sew all four sides together in this manner to form a rectangle. Pin the rectangle to the table-

cloth right sides together and sew, 1/4 in. (1 cm) from the raw edges. Turn the tablecloth right side out, pushing out the mitered corners. Turn under the raw edges of the border and baste them to the back.

Napkins

Cut four pieces of linen 14 x 14 in. (36 x 36 cm). For the borders, cut sixteen pieces of checked fabric 2 x 14-1/4 in. (5 x 36.5 cm).

From the sampler chart, embroider the first and the fourth flower of the top row and the second and the fourth flower of the lower row, one on each of the four napkins. Rotate each flower so its stem points to the corner, about 1 in. (2.5 cm) from the edge. Work each cross-stitch over two threads of linen, using two strands of floss. Outline stitch over completed cross-stitch as for the sampler.

Trim the linen, leaving a 1/4 in. (1 cm) seam allowance all around, so that each napkin is 13-1/4 x 13-1/4 in. (34 x 34 cm).

To make the borders and complete the napkins, follow the directions for the tablecloth borders.

Garden Sampler

*Although we may never see it out our kitchen window,
the manicured, clean-swept symmetry of this formal garden
lends an aura of European elegance to any room.*

Finished Measurements
7-3/4 x 10-1/2 in. (20 x 27 cm)

Materials

A piece of linen 19-1/2 x 27-1/4 in. (50 x 70 cm) with 28 threads per inch (2.5 cm); DMC or Anchor embroidery floss as indicated on the key to the chart plus dark terra cotta #918 or #341; a matching frame.

Directions

Cross-stitch the motif using two strands of floss over two threads of fabric, except on the sky and inside the gate, where you need to use one strand over two threads. Outline stitch over the completed cross-stitch, using one strand of floss, around the flower pots with dark terra cotta #918 or #341 and around all other figures with black. Frame the finished picture.

Key to Chart

		DMC	Anchor			DMC	Anchor
✳	= dark lavender	209	109	−	= light cobalt	828	975
■	= black	310	403	⊞	= dark fawn	840	889
◢	= med. dark salmon	350	11	◺	= light parrot green	906	256
⊿	= salmon	352	9	◣	= emerald	910	229
◟	= very light lime	369	213	◿	= terra cotta	921	338
⊙	= fog	452	233	◥	= med. dark avocado	937	263
▲	= very dark juniper	500	683	⬓	= lime	955	241
●	= dark forest green	561	217	◤	= dark blossom pink	956	54
◺	= blossom pink	605	50	⊠	= light green	988	243
◟	= light cocoa	754	868	◠	= light silver	3024	899
◻	= medium cobalt	809	130	◜	= very light avocado	3348	254
·	= light linen	822	390				

Sampler Trio

$\mathcal{W}$hat's your pleasure? Sailing off into the sunset? Jousting with windmills? A weekend in a country manor? Whether you stitch one, two, or the whole cheerful trio, these small, colorful pictures glow with sunny simplicity, created by combining a few pastels.

Embroidery Measurements
Sailboat: 5 x 5-3/4 in. (13 x 14.5 cm)
Windmill: 6 x 6-3/4 in. (15.5 x 17.5 cm)
House: 8-1/4 x 8-3/4 in. (21.5 x 22.5 cm)

Materials

For each sampler, a piece of linen 2-3/4 in. (7 cm) larger around than the embroidered measurement, with 30 threads per inch (2.5 cm); DMC or Anchor embroidery floss as indicated in the key to the charts plus light gray #415 or #398 and coral #3712 or #1023; a matching frame.

Directions

Using two strands of floss over two threads of linen, cross-stitch the motif, beginning at the lower right corner 2-3/4 in. (7 cm) from the edge of the fabric.

Work in outline stitch over the completed cross-stitch, using one strand of floss: around and in the windows and the doors of the two small houses with azure; around the blades of the windmill with light gray #415 or #398; around the windows of the large house with light cinnamon; and around the door of the large house with azure. For all remaining figures, outline stitch in coral #3712 or #1023. Frame the finished picture.

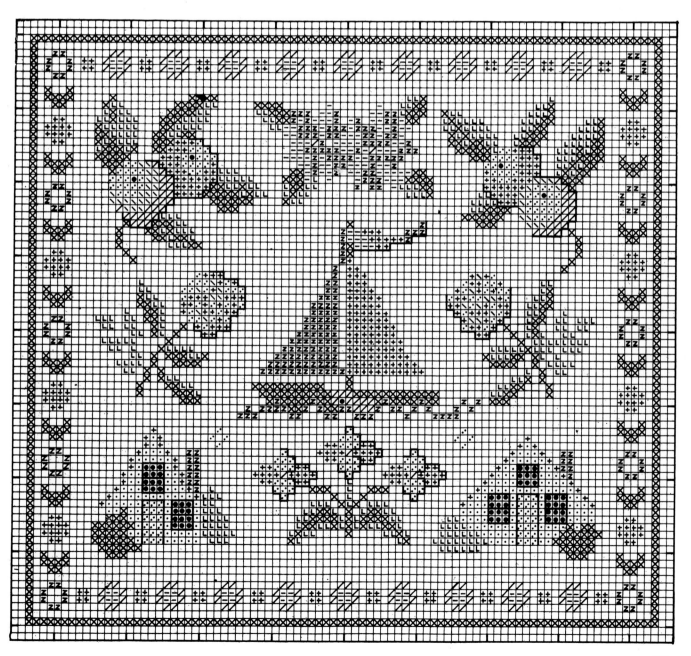

Bears Sampler

You may be tempted to rechristen these bears with names inspired by members of your family or a group of friends…and you may prefer polka dots or tweed or stripes to plaid.

Finished Measurements
21 x 25 in. (54 x 64 cm)
Embroidery Measurements
12-3/4 x 16-3/4 in. (33 x 43 cm)

Materials

29-1/4 x 33 in. (75 x 85 cm) of white linen with 25 threads per inch (2.5 cm); DMC or Anchor embroidery floss as indicated on the key to the chart plus delft #334 or #977; for the mat pictured— plaid fabric 24 x 28 in. (62 x 72 cm), fusible interfacing 20-3/4 x 24-1/2 in. (53 x 63 cm), and a piece of stiff cardboard 20-3/4 x 24-1/2 in. (53 x 63 cm); a wooden frame.

Directions

Begin embroidering at the lower right corner at point A, 8 in. (21 cm) from the edge of the linen. Use two strands of floss, working over two threads of fabric. Using two strands of floss, outline stitch over the completed cross-stitch in a matching shade or one shade darker, in and around the bows, hats, clothes, and bears.

Stem stitch the names of the bears, from upper left to lower right: Teddy, teal; Bert, light pine; Brunno, dark rose; Toby, teal; Peter, medium dark delft; Barend, dark rose; Beer, light pine; and Brom, medium dark delft. Embroider the mouths with two strands of black floss in satin stitch.

To make the mat pictured, cut a 14 x 18 in. (36 x 46 cm) rectangle from the center of the cardboard and discard. Cut fusible interfacing to fit the open cardboard rectangle. Place the interfacing over the cardboard and the plaid fabric over the interfacing and iron together. Trim and fit the fabric to the cardboard, folding under about 1/2 in. (1.5 cm) all around; glue the folded-over fabric to the back of the cardboard as necessary. Mat and frame the finished picture.

Key to Chart

		DMC	Anchor
∙	= white	white	2
▲	= dark rose	309	42
■	= black	310	403
◥	= dark delft	312	979
◹	= medium dark delft	322	978
⊞	= dark gray	414	235
◣	= nutmeg	420	374
◺	= medium nutmeg	422	373
◿	= light toast	436	363
◸	= tan	437	362
▲	= medium pine	502	877
◺	= light pine	503	875
⟋	= light jade	504	213
Z	= gray green	523	859
◺	= medium light teal	598	167
●	= desert	611	898
⟋	= medium linen	642	392
◡	= camel	676	891
◺	= light sand	739	885
◖	= light orange	743	311
◺	= peach	745	300
∙	= light peach	746	275
▼	= teal	807	168
▢	= very light pink	819	271
⠂	= light linen	822	390
⟋	= light delft	828	975
◣	= dark fawn	840	379
⠂	= medium ecru	842	388
○	= light copper	951	366
◺	= dark blush	962	75
◿	= light blush	963	73
◺	= medium light sand	3046	887
◺	= very light turf	3047	852
⊠	= medium copper	3064	369
⠂	= light seafoam	3072	847
◺	= medium light delft	3752	976
◺	= light glacier blue	3756	158
✳	= dark cocoa	3772	371

teddy

ber

peter

karen

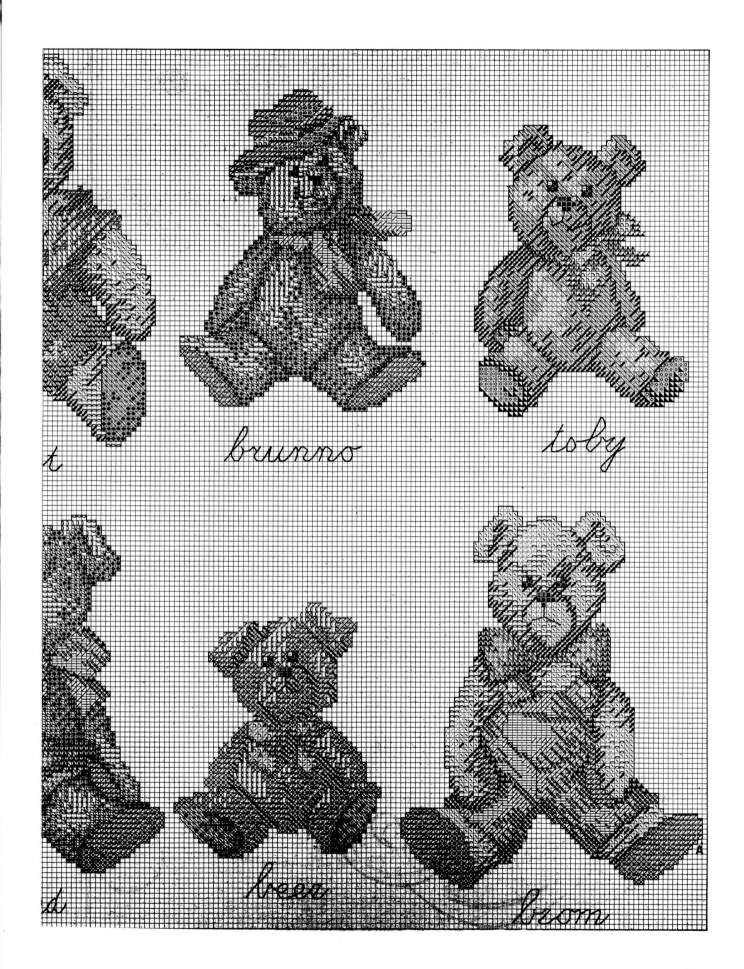

brunno

toby

35

Key to Chart

		DMC	Anchor
⊠	= light cinnamon	402	1047
●	= dark rust	922	1003
▯	= copper	945	881

38

Baby Sampler

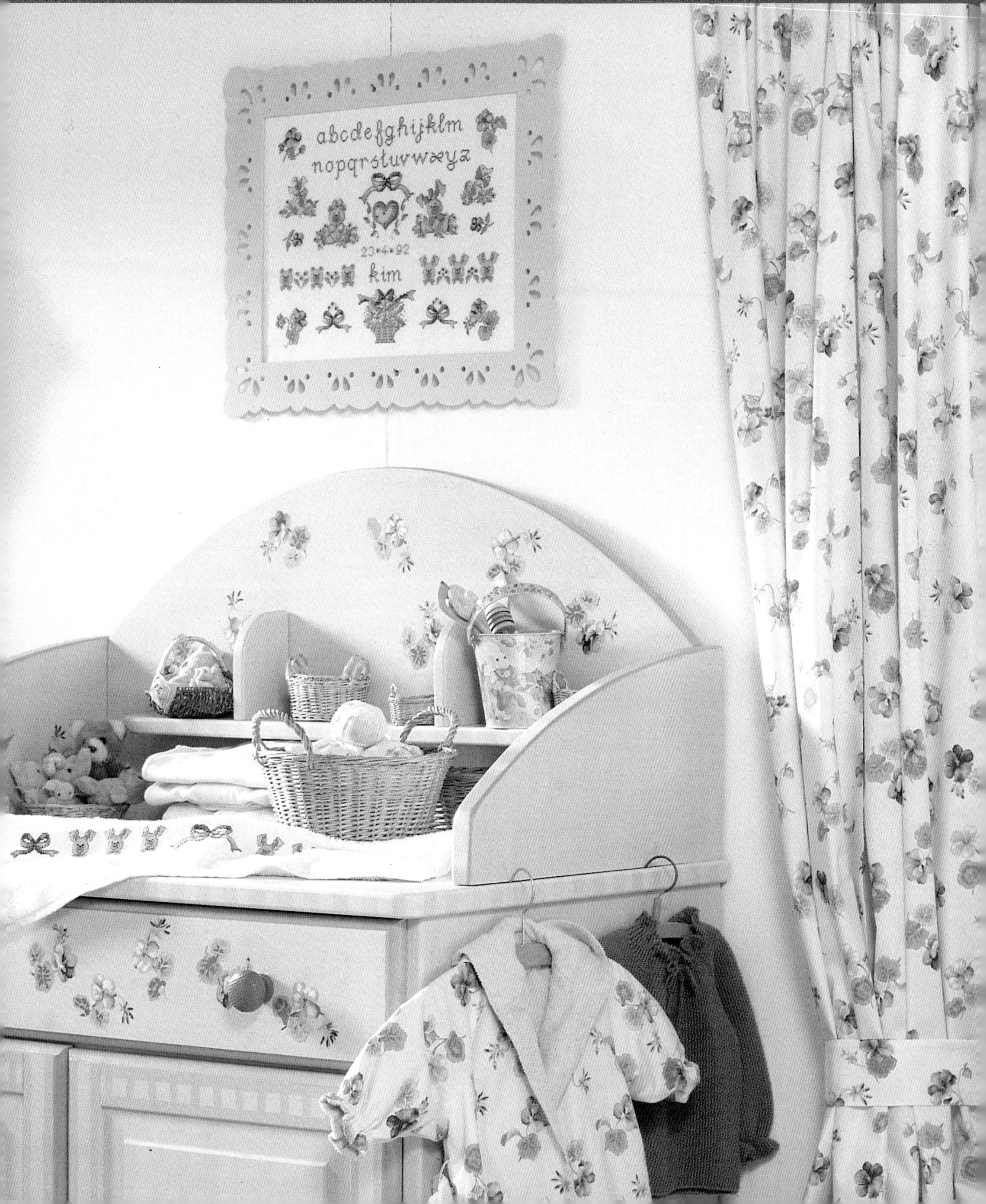

Baby Sampler

A rose is a rose is a rose, wrote Alice B. Toklas, but you don't have to strew them around the baby's room to evoke a feeling of freshness and new beginnings—the whimsical bunnies, bows, and baskets in a sampler like this one create their own rosy bloom.

Finished Measurements
17 x 21 in. (43 x 53 cm)
Embroidery Measurements
10-1/2 x 14 in. (27 x 36 cm)

Materials

19-1/2 x 23-1/2 in. (50 x 60 cm) of linen with 31 threads per inch (2.5 cm); DMC or Anchor embroidery floss as indicated on the key to the chart plus dark red #321 or #47, light navy #797 or #132, dark emerald #699 or #923, and very dark fawn #632 or #936; a matching frame.

Directions

Using two strands of floss over two threads of linen, begin cross-stitching at the lower right corner at point A, 4-3/4 in. (12.5 cm) from the edge. Center the numbers of the birth date and the baby's name in the spaces as indicated in the photo.

Use one strand of floss for outline stitching. Using a darker shade than the embroidered color, outline stitch around each figure in dark red #321 or #47, light navy #797 or #132, dark emerald #699 or #923, or very dark fawn #632 or #936. Work outline stitch between the leaves next to the centers of the flowers in medium mint green. Work satin stitch using two strands of floss: in dark emerald #699 or #923 for the leaves, charcoal for the mouths, and dark magenta where circles appear on the chart.

Frame the finished picture.

Key to Chart		DMC	Anchor
= jade		320	215
= medium wheat		422	943
= tan		437	362
= dark magenta		602	63
= light camel		729	890
= light wheat		738	942
= light sand		739	885
= light cobalt		775	128
= light ocean blue		794	175
= dark cobalt		798	131
= very light pink		819	271
= medium mint green		913	204
= light spice		951	366
= medium turquoise		958	187
= light lime		966	240
= light rust		977	363
= light raspberry		3688	66
= light blossom pink		3689	49
= very light cherry		3708	31
= charcoal		3799	236

Cactus Sampler

These delicate flowers growing from spiny cactuses are reminders

that the unexpected has its own special beauty—

that in time even a desert blooms.

Embroidery Measurements
7-3/4 x 18 in. (20 x 46 cm)

Materials
Linen fabric 15-1/2 x 25-1/4 in. (40 x 65 cm) with 26 threads per inch (2.5 cm); DMC or Anchor embroidery floss as indicated on the key to the chart; matching frame.

Directions
Begin embroidering cactus 1 at the lower right corner at point A, 6 in. (15 cm) from the side and lower edge. Work all stitches over two threads, using two strands of floss for cross-stitch and one strand for outline stitch, unless otherwise indicated.

Begin embroidering cactuses 2, 3, 4, and 5 on the same row of threads at which you began cactus 1; leave 52 threads between cactuses 1 and 2, 62 threads between cactuses 2 and 3, 56 threads between cactuses 3 and 4, and 60 threads between cactuses 4 and 5.

Outline stitch cactus 1 with dark green, along the top of the pot with dark rust, along the sides of the pot with very dark fawn, and along the flowers with light lavender. Stem stitch the thorns in the middle of the cactus with very light beige and the thorns around the cactus with dark rust.

On cactus 2, outline stitch in and around the flower with light maroon, in and around the cactus with dark green, and in and around the flower pot and the dish with very dark fawn. Stem stitch the thorns with two strands of white.

Outline stitch in and around the flower on cactus 3 with medium sand, along the dish and the top of the pot with very dark fawn, along the sides of the pot with dark rust, along the sides of the cactus with dark chartreuse, and along the top of the cactus with dark green. Stem stitch the thorns using two strands of dark rust, and stem stitch the centers using two strands of medium peach.

Outline stitch around cactus 4 with dark green, along the top and lower edge of the flower pot with very dark fawn, and along the sides of the pot and the dish with dark rust. Stem stitch the thorns with dark rust.

Stem stitch in and around the flowers on cactus 5 with dark fuchsia, around the pot with very dark fawn, and along the dish with dark rust. Stem stitch the thorns with dark rust.

Frame the finished picture.

Cactus 3

Key to Chart

		DMC	Anchor			DMC	Anchor
⋅	= white	white	2	∣	= light cocoa	754	1012
◣	= light lavender	210	108	◹	= medium light coral	760	1022
◿	= lavender	211	342	◢	= dark fuchsia	891	29
●	= dark brick	355	1014	⋅⋅	= dark rust	922	1003
�₋	= medium jade	368	214	∴	= very light beige	948	1011
◿	= very light lime	369	1043	◸	= light maroon	961	76
◠	= light cinnamon	402	1047	◣	= dark green	986	246
Z	= medium dark beige	407	914	◸	= light green	988	243
⊘	= dark chartreuse	470	255	⊠	= medium lime	989	242
◡	= light chartreuse	472	253	✳	= medium sand	3045	888
◤	= medium dark sand	610	889	⊤	= medium light sand	3046	887
◥	= desert	611	898	⊙	= med. lt. loden green	3053	261
▲	= very dark fawn	632	936	◺	= very light jonquil	3078	292
◹	= medium peach	744	301	◺	= blush	3354	74

43

Cactus 1

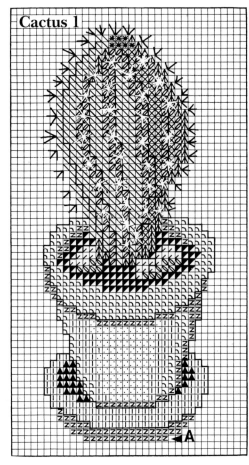

Cactus 2

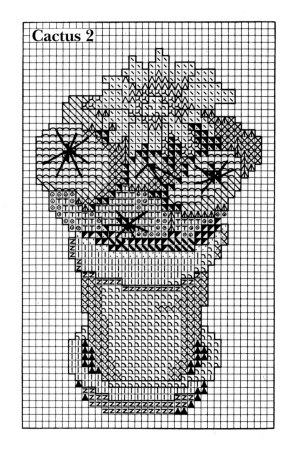

Cactus 4

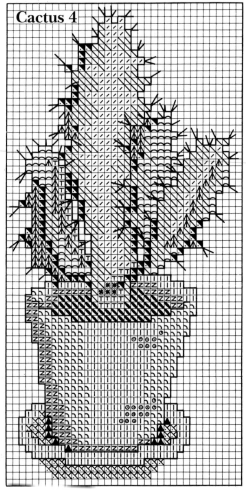

Cactus 5

Wildflowers Sampler

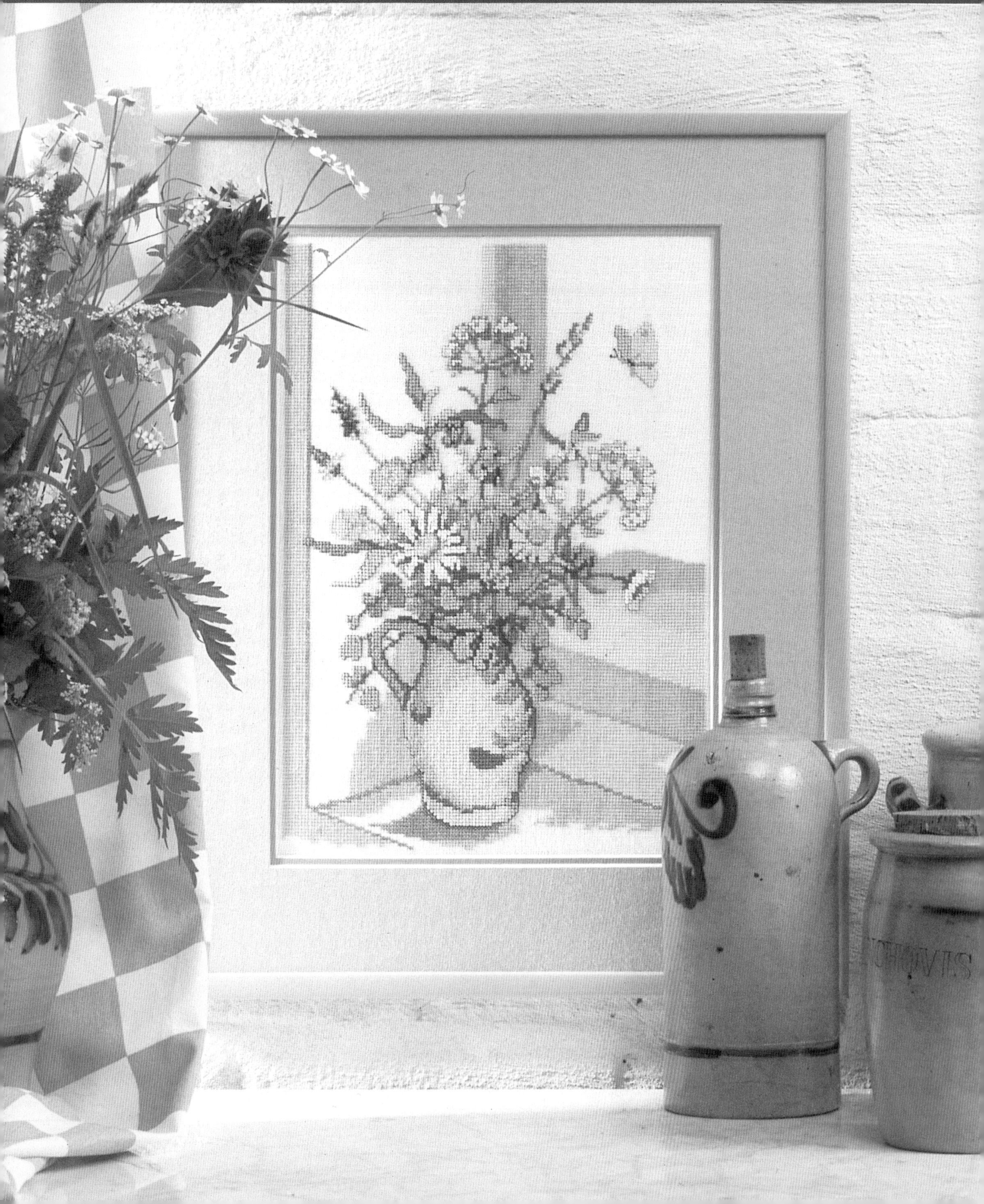

Wildflowers Sampler

Daisies…Queen Anne's lace…buttercups…a cloudless sky…green hills…sunshine—no wonder novelist Henry James thought "summer afternoon" the most beautiful phrase in the English language. With this pleasing pastel in your home, you throw open the window to summer all year long.

Finished Measurements
16-1/2 x 20 in. (42 x 51 cm)
Embroidery Measurements
9-3/4 x 13-1/2 in. (25 x 35 cm)

Materials
25-1/4 x 29-1/4 in. (65 x 75 cm) of linen with 25 threads per inch (2.5 cm); DMC or Anchor embroidery floss as indicated on the key to the chart; a matching frame and double mat.

Directions
Begin at the lower right at point A, 7-3/4 in. (20 cm) from the edges of the linen, and cross-stitch the motif according to the chart, working each stitch over two threads of fabric. Use one strand of floss for the back-ground, two strands for the gray shadows of the vase, and three strands for the blue shades in the vase, the flowers, and the window frame.

Work in outline stitch over the completed cross-stitch, using one strand of floss: medium lime around the light lime butterfly wings; light orange around the medium peach butterfly wings; medium light green around the white flowers; light navy around the vase; medium watermelon around the lilac flowers; and a matching shade or a shade darker around the remaining figures.

Mat and frame the finished picture.

Key to Chart

Symbol	Color	DMC	Anchor
⋅	= white	white	2
■	= dark watermelon	309	39
⊘	= gray	318	399
◺	= medium watermelon	335	38
◻	= medium jade	368	214
⌣	= light gray	415	398
▲	= nutmeg	420	374
∷	= light yellow	445	288
∨	= light chartreuse	472	253
‖	= light azure	519	1038
▲	= light violet	553	98
◲	= lilac	554	96
▼	= medium dark sand	610	889
○	= orange	742	303
∧	= light orange	743	302
−	= medium peach	744	301
◿	= silver	762	234
◹	= pink	776	24
■	= light navy	797	132
∨	= dark cobalt	798	131
◺	= light indigo	800	144
⌐	= medium cobalt	809	130
∴	= light pink	818	23
Z	= medium saffron	834	874
◣	= dark rust	922	1003
◿	= light lime	966	240
╱	= medium light green	987	244
●	= light green	988	243
●	= medium lime	989	242
◠	= light watermelon	3326	36
⊠	= med. light avocado	3347	266
‖	= very light avocado	3348	264

Farmyard Sampler

*The tidiness and abundance of this scene seem to beg
to be set to music…ten tulips glowing, eight gardens growing,
four trees ablooming, three rabbits hopping, two chickens pecking,
one rooster crowing… A project this large could easily be a group endeavor.*

Finished Measurements
52-1/2 x 38-1/4 in. (135 x 98 cm)

Materials
1-3/4 yd. (1.55 m) unbleached linen 54-1/2 in. (140 cm) wide with 13 threads per inch (2.5 cm); DMC tapestry wool as indicated on the key to the chart plus dark bark #7700, light rosebud pink #7804, and dark magenta #7603; a piece of chipboard 52-1/2 x 38-1/4 in. (135 x 98 cm).

Note: To make the entire sampler smaller and finer, use linen with more threads per inch and DMC or Anchor embroidery floss as listed in the key to the chart plus dark bark #400 or #351, light rosebud pink #604 or #55, and dark magenta #602 or #63.

Directions
Working each cross-stitch with two strands of yarn over two threads of linen, embroider the motif according to the chart. Begin at point A, 8-1/2 in. (22 cm) from the lower edge and 5-3/4 in. (15 cm) from the side edges.

For the border, work in satin stitch over three threads using three shades of green: the outside edge in light green, the center in medium green, and the inside edge in green. Outline the gardens in satin stitch over two threads using medium green. Embroider the fence with dark bark #7700 (embroidery floss #400 or #351) with large satin stitches and horizontal stem stitches. Embroider the path to the house by working vertical running stitches with ecru wool, then working through these with whipped running stitches using gray wool. For the gate, work in alternating long and short straight stitches (see chart) with light blue.

Finish in outline stitch when other embroidery is complete. Outline the pigs in dark magenta #7603 (#602 or #63); the sheep in dark brown; the yellow flowers in orange; the hen, chickens, and chicks in red; the cats in white; and the people and the tails of the rabbits in black. Stem stitch the clothesline in black and the tails of the pigs in light rosebud pink #7804 (#604 or #55).

Stretch the embroidery over the chipboard and tack in place.

Key to Chart

		DMC Tapestry Wool	DMC Floss	Anchor Floss
·	= white	white	white	2
	= ecru	ecru	ecru	387
◣	= black	black	310	403
▲	= dark red	7110	816	20
⊙	= pink	7122	950	4146
⁄	= dark pink	7133	776	24
◹	= brown	7171	951	880
⁄	= light green	7341	907	255
⁄·	= medium green	7342	906	256
◺	= green	7344	905	257
◗	= dark green	7346	986	246
⁄	= yellow	7435	307	289
⬝·	= dark beige	7465	841	378
●	= dark brown	7469	838	380
⊠	= medium red	7544	304	19
⊡	= gray	7618	318	399
X	= red	7666	666	46
	= beige	7739	738	361
⋁	= light orange	7741	741	304
◖	= soft green	7772	3348	264
⁄	= blue	7797	797	132
◺	= light blue	7799	800	144
▼	= orange	7947	971	316
◿	= orange yellow	7971	972	298

HOME AND HEARTH
Windmill Cushions

*Nearly as dazzling as the scarlet tulips in the background,
these cushions will brighten a room or a mood. And with no color
police to check up on you (no law mandates light blue skies, for
instance), you can stitch them in whatever combinations you choose.*

Finished Measurements

20-1/2 x 20-1/2 in. (52.5 x 52.5 cm)

Materials

For each cushion, double-threaded rug canvas 23-1/2 x 23-1/2 in. (60 x 60 cm) with 18 squares per 4 in. (10 cm); 2-1/2 yd. (2.25 m) of seam binding; worsted-weight cotton yarn as indicated on the key to the chart; a piece of green cotton 22 x 29 in. (56.5 x 74.5 cm); a pillow form 20 x 20 in. (51 x 51 cm); masking tape (optional).

Directions

Cover the edges of the rug canvas with seam binding or masking tape to prevent raveling. Cross-stitch your chosen motif according to its chart, working each stitch with one strand of cotton over one double-thread crossing. Begin at the lower right, 2 in. (5 cm) from the edge. When you've completed the motif, trim the canvas 3/4 in. (2 cm) from the edges of your embroidery.

For the back of the cushion, cut two pieces of green cloth 14-1/2 x 22 in. (37 x 56.5 cm). Make a hem 1 in. (2.5 cm) wide with a 1/4 in. (1 cm) inner hem along one long side of each back piece.

Key to Charts

1 = white

2 = green

3 = brown

4 = light blue

5 = purple

6 = pink

7 = red

8 = rust

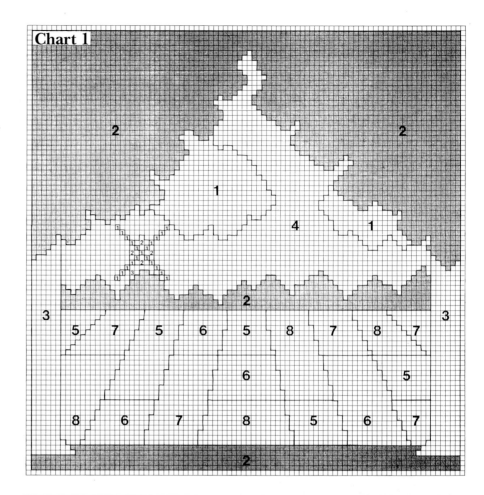

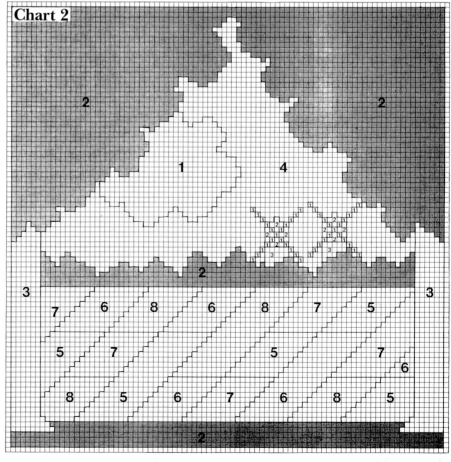

Overlap the hemmed edges and
tack in place so that the back is
the same size as the front. With
right sides together, sew around
the edges of the back and front
1 in. (2.5 cm) from your embroidery. Turn right side out. Insert
the pillow form.

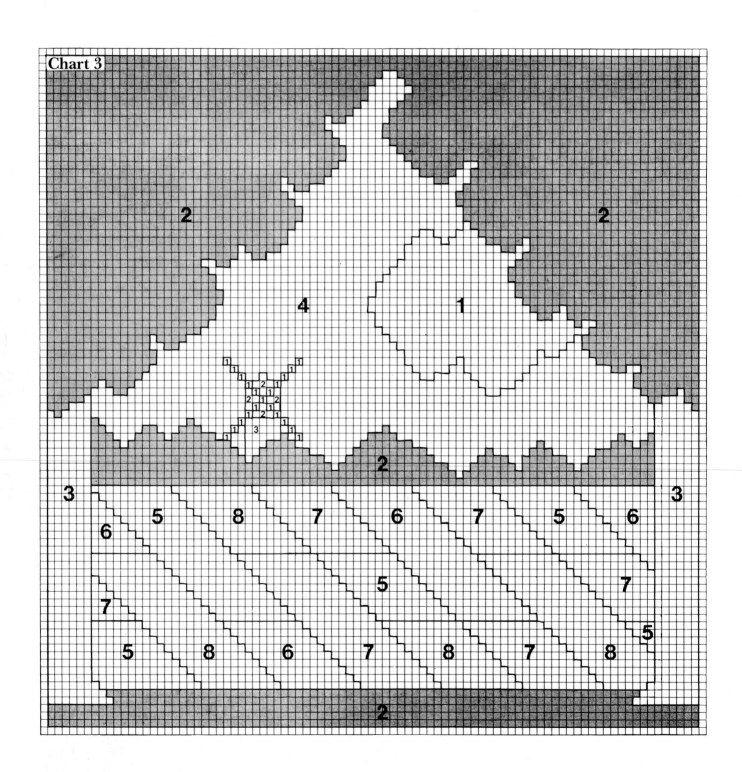

Chart 3

54

Pansies Sampler

Along a walk or on a wall, the velvety faces of pansies combine

the old-fashioned charm of tea roses, the delicacy of violets,

and the cheerfulness of daisies—an entire garden on their own.

Finished Measurements
13-1/2 x 15-1/4 in. (35 x 39 cm)
Embroidery Measurements
8-1/2 x 11-1/4 in. (22 x 29 cm)

Materials

21-1/2 x 23-1/2 in. (55 x 60 cm) of ecru linen with 25 threads per inch (2.5 cm); DMC or Anchor embroidery floss as indicated in the key to the chart plus black #310 or #403, green #986 or #245, and charcoal #3799 or #236.

Directions

Working each cross-stitch with two strands of floss over two threads of linen, begin at the lower right corner at point A, 6-1/4 in. (16 cm) from the lower edge (long side) of the linen and 9-3/4 in. (25 cm) from the right edge. Embroider the motif according to the chart.

Work in outline stitch over the completed cross-stitch, using one strand of floss: around the pansies in very dark violet, the leaves in green #986 or #245, the vase in charcoal #3799 or #236, and the centers of the pansies in black #310 or #403. Frame the finished picture.

Key to Chart

		DMC	Anchor
	= white	white	2
	= light purple	208	110
	= dark lavender	209	109
	= light lavender	210	108
	= dark grape	333	119
	= delft	334	977
	= medium avocado	469	267
	= gray green	522	860
	= med. light gray green	523	859
	= light gray green	524	858
	= very dark violet	550	102
	= violet	552	99
	= light violet	553	98
	= lilac	554	96
	= very lt. desert (1 strand)	644	830
	= camel	676	891
	= very light ecru	712	926
	= med. light tangerine	741	313
	= light tangerine	742	311
	= medium peach	744	301
	= peach	745	300
	= light peach	746	386
	= medium light copper	758	882
	= silver	762	234
	= very lt. loden green	772	259
	= medium ocean blue	792	177
	= light indigo	800	144
	= dark seafoam	927	848
	= light copper	951	880
	= very lt. turf (1 strand)	3047	852
	= med. lt. loden green	3053	261
	= light seafoam	3072	847
	= v. lt. jonquil (1 strand)	3078	292
	= medium melon	3340	329
	= light loden green	3364	260
	= medium orchid	3607	87
	= medium light orchid	3608	86
	= light lilac	3609	95
	= dark raspberry	3685	70
	= light carmine	3689	48
	= light fawn	3774	376

Pansies Rug

Instead of a red carpet, roll out this pansies rug

for special guests—perfect at the front door,

as a bedroom or bath accent, or as an area rug.

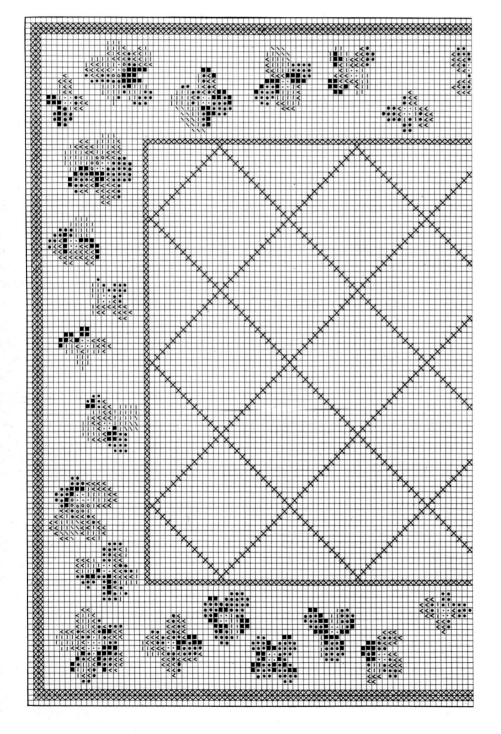

Finished Measurements
37 x 44-3/4 in. (95 x 115 cm)

Materials

1-1/4 yd. (1.1 m) of rug canvas 58-1/2 in. (150 cm) wide with 13 squares per 4 in. (10 cm); Anchor rug wool, or its equivalent, as indicated on the key to the chart; 4-3/4 yd. (4.3 m) of seam binding 1-1/2 in. (4 cm) wide.

Directions

Edge the canvas in seam binding or tape to keep it from raveling. Using one strand of wool over one double-thread crossing, cross-stitch the motif according to the chart, beginning 2-1/4 in. (6 cm) from the lower right corner of the canvas. Work the outlines in gray blue and the background in light beige. Trim the finished rug, leaving 1-1/2 in. (4 cm) of canvas beyond the embroidery all the way around. Sew seam binding along the edges, fold the edges under, and sew them to the back.

Key to Chart

		Anchor Rug Wool	No. of Skeins
■	= bright blue	3032	1
V	= blue	3107	1
●	= dark blue	3109	1
–	= light blue	3145	1
⊠	= gray blue	3146	3
□	= light beige	3205	16
·	= yellow	3208	1
⧄	= lilac	3225	1
○	= yellow orange	3261	1

Materials

An ecru cotton throw; 31 x 31 in. (.8 x .8 m) of linen with 13 threads per inch (2.5 cm); tapestry wool as indicated in the key to the chart plus light burgundy #8524, burgundy #8526, dark burgundy #8528, very dark purple #8612, dark green #9006, and black #9800.

Directions

Cut four pieces of linen 15-1/2 x 15-1/2 in. (40 x 40 cm). Pin a square in each corner of the throw 1-1/4 in. (3.5 cm) from each edge. Begin embroidering 3 in. (7.5 cm) from the edge of the throw and cross-stitch through the linen and the throw, using one strand of wool over four threads.

Embroider the pansy in blue violet on a diagonal in two opposite corners according to the key to the chart. In the other two corners, embroider the pansy on a diagonal in shades of burgundy, substituting light burgundy #8524 for light violet, burgundy #8526 for violet, and dark burgundy #8528 for dark violet. Work in outline stitch over the completed cross-stitch, around the petals in very dark purple #8612, the leaves in dark green #9006, and the centers in black #9800. Trim away the excess linen around the completed embroidery.

It's doubly satisfying to create something practical that is also gorgeous…Great for curling up on winter evenings in front of the fire, for naps on long, rainy afternoons, for picnics by the lake.

Embroidery Measurements
13-1/2 x 13-1/2 in. (35 x 35 cm)

Key to Chart

	Anchor Tapestry Wool			Anchor Tapestry Wool
· = ecru	8004		= violet	8608
= light yellow	8056		= dark violet	8610
v = yellow	8120		= green	9004
= orange	8166		+ = moss green	9020
● = purple	8592		· = light green	9172
= dark purple	8596		= light rust	9620
= light violet	8604			

Hen Table Linens

*Doesn't this bread cloth conjure up spring Sunday mornings—
and call out for homemade biscuits and strawberry jam? Or maybe
cinnamon toast? Or blueberry muffins? And matching egg warmers,
like tea cozies, grapefruit spoons, and real cream, surely stand for
pampered living—or at least for a luxurious breakfast table.*

Bread Cloth
Finished Measurements
16-3/4 x 16-3/4 in. (43 x 43 cm)

Egg Warmer
Finished Measurements
3-3/4 in. (9.5 cm) high

Materials

For the bread cloth, white Aida or Hardanger fabric 17-1/2 x 17-1/2 in. (45 x 45 cm) with 11-1/2 thread groups per inch (2.5 cm) and 2 yd. (1.75 m) of bias seam binding; for each egg warmer, white Aida or Hardanger fabric 6 x 11-3/4 in. (15 x 30 cm) with 11-1/2 thread groups per inch (2.5 cm) and pieces of white cotton and of felt 4-1/4 x 9-1/4 in. (11 x 24 cm); for all linens, DMC or Anchor embroidery floss as indicated on the key to the chart plus medium blue #798 or #142.

Directions
Bread Cloth

Trim the fabric to 16-3/4 x 16-3/4 in. (43 x 43 cm), being care-ful to make the threads straight on all edges. Sew bias seam binding along the edges. Embroider one hen in the center of each corner so that two hens' beaks point toward each other on each side of the cloth. Work cross-stitch using three strands of floss over one thread group. Using two strands of floss, outline stitch over completed cross-stitch, in and around the blue flowers with medium blue #798 or #142 and around the hens with light topaz.

Egg Warmer

Make a paper pattern from the outline provided. From the pattern, cut two pieces each of Aida cloth, felt, and cotton; add one inch (2.5 cm) at the bottom of the pattern for the Aida cloth for the hem.

Using three strands of floss over one thread group, cross-stitch the motif on the Aida cloth according to the chart. Embroider a row of cross-stitch-es 1/4 in. (1 cm) from the hem-line (see the photo). Outline

		DMC	Anchor
·	= white	white	2
■	= black	310	403
	= light grape	341	117
T	= medium jade	368	214
	= medium nutmeg	422	373
	= very light desert	644	830
	= pewter	647	1040
o	= medium light jonquil	726	295
	= light sand	739	885
—	= light cobalt	775	128
	= light topaz	783	307
	= ocean blue	793	176
	= medium mint green	913	204
	= lime	955	241
✳	= dark blush	962	75
X	= medium lime	989	242
	= peacock blue	996	433

Key to Chart

BREAD CLOTH

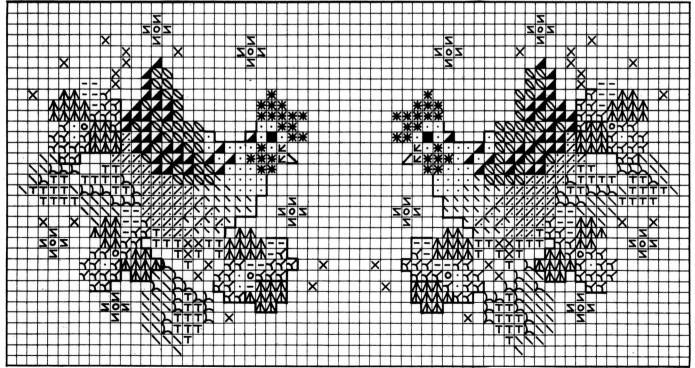

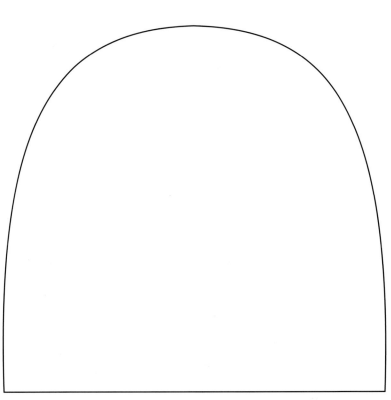

EGG WARMER PATTERN

EGG WARMER

stitch over completed cross-stitch, in and around the blue flowers with medium blue #798 or #142 and around the hen with light topaz. Use two strands of ocean blue floss for the antenna of the butterfly and for a French knot at the end of each antenna.

Pin the two pieces of Aida cloth right sides together and sew around the sides 1/4 in. (1 cm) from the edge, leaving the bottom edge open. Turn right side out. Layer the two pieces of felt lining with the two pieces of cotton between them and pin. Sew as for the Aida cloth. Trim the edges and insert the lining inside the Aida cloth. Turn the Aida cloth hem under and slip-stitch over the lining and felt.

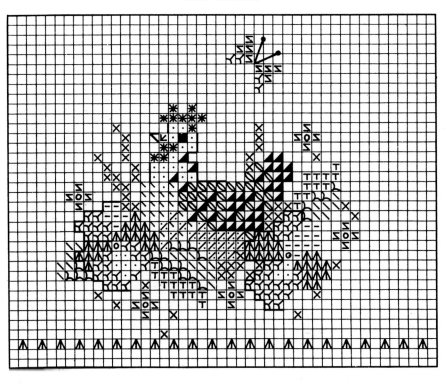

64

Patchwork Pillow

*Combining the richness of tapestry with the charm of patchwork,
this cross-stitched cushion has an elegance all its own. As with potato
chips or chocolates, the real challenge may be to stop after just one.*

Patchwork Pillow

Finished Measurements
13-1/2 x 13-1/2 in. (35 x 35 cm)

Materials
19-1/2 x 19-1/2 in. (50 x 50 cm) of canvas with 13 double threads per inch (2.5 cm); 19-1/2 x 19-1/2 in. (50 x 50 cm) of cotton for the back; stuffing or a pillow form; DMC pearl cotton, or its equivalent, as indicated in the key to the chart.

Directions
Begin cross-stitch 2 in. (5 cm) from the edge of the canvas, using all six strands of pearl cotton over one double-thread crossing. Block the embroidered piece.

To make the pillow, place the cotton and the embroidered piece right sides together and sew around three edges, allowing a 3/4 in. (2 cm) seam. Trim the seams and turn the pillowcase right side out. Insert the pillow form or stuffing and sew the last side closed.

Key to Chart
DMC Pearl Cotton

Symbol	Color	Number
◉	= purple	315
●	= red	321
○	= rose red	351
◯	= pale pink	353
✚	= light green	369
⊠	= light yellow green	472
▢	= light gray green	504
✗	= bright green	703
▢	= cream	712
⊠	= dark yellow	742
✕	= yellow	743
○	= old rose	760
▲	= blue	799
△	= light blue	800
✚	= gray blue	926
✖	= orange	970
✕	= lime	993
⊙	= pink	3326

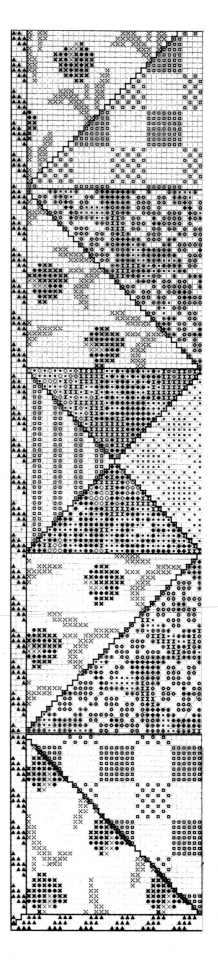

67

Red Cushion

A clutch of bright cushions brings fresh life to a couch, a futon, a bed—the beauty of this design lies in its simplicity and the endless number of variations it allows. Ecru and cranberry aren't for you? How about cream and cobalt? Peach and charcoal? Rust and gold?

Finished Measurements
14-1/2 x 14-1/2 in. (37 x 37 cm)

Materials

1/2 yd (.45 m) of ecru linen 54-1/2 in. (140 cm) wide with 30 threads per inch (2.5 cm); dark red embroidery floss (DMC #321 or Anchor #47); ecru sewing machine thread; a pillow form 14 x 14 in. (36 x 36 cm).

Directions

Cut a piece of linen 18 x 18 in. (46 x 46 cm) for the front of the pillow. Working with three strands of embroidery floss over three threads of linen, embroider the front in cross-stitch according to the chart, beginning at the lower right corner 2 in. (5 cm) from the edge. Repeat the chart for the second half of the cushion. Trim the fabric 1-1/2 in. (4 cm) from the embroidery.

Cut two pieces 11 x 15 in. (28 x 38.5 cm) for the back. Make a hem 1 in. (2.5 cm) wide with a 1/4 in. (1 cm) inner hem along one long side of each back piece. Overlap the hemmed edges and tack in place so that the back is the same size as the front: 14 x 14 in. (36 x 36 cm). With right sides together, sew around the edges of the back and front 1 in. (2.5 cm) from your embroidery. Turn right side out. Insert the pillow form.

Seashore Table Linens

*Even without a salt-water aquarium, much less a beach house,
one can find the variety and symmetry of ocean creatures fascinating.
Although perfect for a table top, this wreath of edible and
nonedible gifts from the sea would also look handsome
framed behind a shell or beach collection.*

Tablecloth Finished Measurements
59 x 59 in. (150 x 150 cm)
Tablecloth Embroidery Measurements
21-1/2 in. (55 cm)
Napkin Finished Measurements
14 x 14 in. (36 x 36 cm)

Materials

For the tablecloth, 1-3/4 yd. (1.6 m), and for each napkin, 17 x 17 in. (44 x 44 cm), of pink-and-white-checked Hardanger cloth 63 in. (160 cm) wide with 23 double threads per inch (2.5 cm); DMC or Anchor embroidery floss as indicated on the key to the chart plus medium watermelon #335 or #38 and light red #349 or #46; and DMC or Anchor embroidery floss or pearl cotton #5 in light coral #761 or #1021, dark antique blue #932 or #1033, and light linen #822 or #390.

Directions
Tablecloth

Mark the horizontal and vertical center of the cloth with a few basting stitches. Center the chart at point M. Using two strands of floss for each cross-stitch over two double thread groups, repeat the motif around the cloth, as shown in the photo.

Outline stitch over the completed cross-stitch using two strands of floss: light red #349 or #46 around the crabs and the starfish; medium watermelon

#335 or #38 around the light pink and light plum shells; and light charcoal around the other shells.

Making sure that you cut between thread groups, trim the fabric to a square 62 x 62 (158 x 158 cm). Use three strands of floss or pearl cotton to edge the tablecloth with three rows of running whipstitching, each row separated by two to four thread groups. (A running whipstitch is a continuous whipstitch, a decorative stitch that in this case does not join two pieces of fabric.) Work the outside row in dark antique blue #932 or #1033 three blocks from the edge; use light linen #822 or #390 for the second row and light coral #761 or #1021 for the third. Make a hem one block wide with an inner hem.

Napkins

For one napkin, cross-stitch three shell motifs from the tablecloth in one corner, 3-1/4 in. (8.5 cm) from the edges, using two strands of floss over two double thread groups. Outline stitch as for the tablecloth. For the border, embroider a row of running

whipstitching three blocks from the edge, using three strands of light coral floss or pearl cotton #761 or #1021. Make a hem one block wide with an inner hem.

Key to Chart		DMC	Anchor
·	= white	white	1
◥	= black	310	403
✳	= medium mauve	316	1017
⊠	= light charcoal	317	400
◿	= gray	318	399
◩	= light gray	415	398
●	= nutmeg	420	374
⬓	= tan	437	362
◗	= very light fawn	543	933
⊥	= medium desert	612	832
◺	= camel	676	891
⊟	= very light ecru	712	926
◺	= light apricot	722	323
◹	= light nutmeg	738	372
◖	= light sand	739	885
◿	= light plum	778	968
◺	= light pink	819	271
◸	= dark rust	922	1003
◿	= light slate	931	1034
◺	= light blush	963	73
◹	= light rust	977	1002
◺	= amethyst	3042	870
◿	= light seafoam	3072	847
⬓	= light watermelon	3326	36
◩	= medium melon	3340	329
◺	= light melon	3341	328

Oven Mitt

From the gourmet cook to the domestically impaired,

who doesn't appreciate sturdy, handsome kitchen accessories?

76

Finished Measurements
9-1/4 x 7 in. (24 x 18 cm)

Materials

One piece of ecru fabric with 22 thread groups per inch (2.5 cm), one piece of unbleached cotton for the lining, and one piece of felt for the inner lining, each 9-3/4 x 23-1/2 in. (25 x 60 cm); DMC or Anchor embroidery floss as indicated on the key to the chart.

Directions

Make a paper pattern for the mitt, using the graph. Cut two pieces each of ecru fabric, felt, and cotton from the pattern, allowing for a 1/4 in. (1 cm) seam; for the ecru only, also allow a 3/4 in. (2 cm) hem. Center the motif on the ecru fabric and cross-stitch, using two strands of floss over two threads of fabric.

Stack all six pieces of fabric: sandwich the ecru fabric right sides together between the felt pieces, and lay the cotton pieces on the top and bottom. Stitch around the outside of the mitt, sewing through all six layers 1/4 inch (1 cm) from the edge and leaving the bottom open. To prevent fraying, finish the edge with a machine zigzag stitch or whipstitch. Fold the ecru hem over and stitch into place. Turn the mitt right side out.

Cut out a 1 x 4 in. (2.5 x 10 cm) strip of ecru fabric for the hanging loop. Fold the strip in half lengthwise with right sides together and sew along the length. Turn right side out and top stitch along the seamed edge. Fold the loop in half and sew the ends to the inside corner of the mitt.

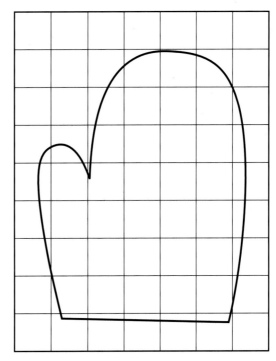

1 SQUARE = 1-1/2 IN. (4 CM)

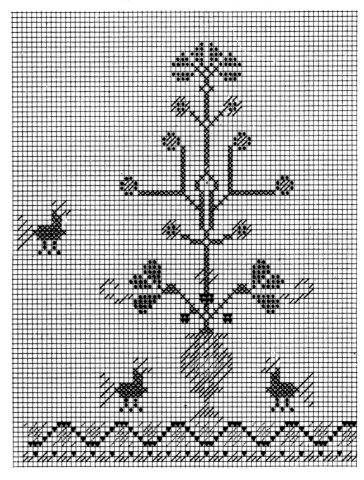

Key to Chart

		DMC	Anchor
▼	= dark pine	500	879
⊠	= medium dark pine	501	878
⠂	= pine	503	876
╱	= dark fawn	840	379
•	= slate	930	1035

Pincushion

A tiny patchwork mosaic, this pincushion could as readily become a sachet or a Christmas-tree decoration, an easy-to-make gift that could be personalized with favorite colors and scents.

Finished Measurements
3 x 3-1/4 in. (8 x 8.5 cm)

Materials

5-1/2 x 5-1/2 in. (14 x 14 cm) of white linen with 30 threads per inch (2.5 cm); DMC or Anchor embroidery floss as indicated on the key to the chart; cotton fabric 5-1/2 x 5-1/2 in. (14 x 14 cm); fiberfill.

Directions

Using two strands of floss over two threads of linen, cross-stitch according to the chart, beginning at the lower right corner, 3/4 in. (2 cm) from the edge. Trim the linen 1/4 in. (1 cm) beyond the embroidery. Cut the cotton fabric for the back the same size as the trimmed embroidered piece. Place the back and front right sides together and sew a 1/4 in. (1 cm) seam around three edges. Trim the corners and turn right side out. Stuff the pin cushion and sew the opening closed.

Braid the remaining very light ecru, light fog, and medium jonquil floss into four cords, each 4-3/4 in. (12 cm) long. Sew the cords along the edges of the pincushion. Knot a cord at each corner and trim the ends, as in the photo.

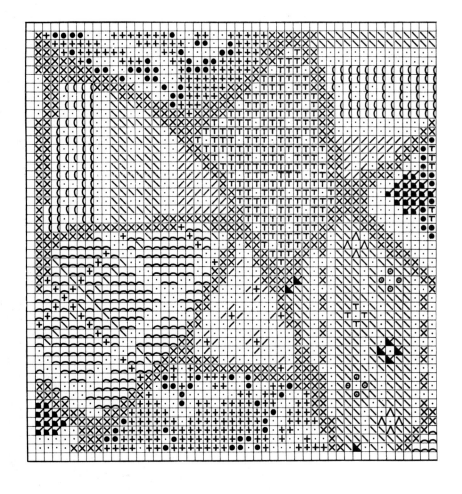

Key to Chart		
Color	**DMC**	**Anchor**
◸ = medium mauve	316	1017
● = medium dark coral	347	1025
T = salmon	352	9
⊠ = dark fog	451	233
◡ = light fog	453	231
◿ = azure	518	1039
◤ = red orange	606	335
· = very light ecru	712	926
◖ = medium light jonquil	726	295
+ = med. lt. terra cotta	758	337
⊙ = medium jonquil	973	297
◣ = med. loden green	3052	262
◺ = med. lt. loden green	3053	261

Shell Towels

*One of the attractions of these towels lies in deciding which
of the nearly infinite variety of ocean-related color combinations
to choose—sea green towels with pale peach shells,
ecru with terra cotta, teal with cream…*

Embroidery Measurements
Each shell, 1-1/2 x 1-3/4 in. (4 x 4.5 cm)

Materials

A hand towel; a piece of unbleached Hardanger fabric 2-1/4 in. (6 cm) wide with 25 double threads per inch (2.5 cm); and DMC or Anchor embroidery floss as indicated on the key to the chart plus medium mauve #316 or #1017.

Directions

Evenly space the three shell motifs on the Hardanger fabric. For each cross-stitch, use two strands of floss over two thread groups of fabric. Outline stitch over completed cross-stitch, using one strand of medium mauve #316 or #1017.

To finish, make a small hem around all edges of the Hardanger fabric and sew the fabric across one end of the towel, as shown.

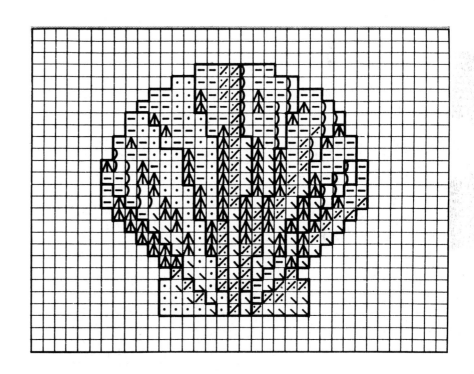

Key to Chart

		DMC	Anchor
·	= white	white	2
◁	= wine	224	893
⊡	= light tan	738	361
◣	= light sand	739	885
)	= silver	762	234
▭	= light plum	778	968

Country Cushions

These patchwork cushions reflect the best of a family—love, comfort, security, joy. The plaids set off the cross-stitch especially well, but an entirely different mood could be created with velvets or flowered prints.

Embroidery Measurements
11-3/4 x 11-3/4 in. to 13-1/2 x 13-1/2 in.
(30 x 30 cm to 35 x 35 cm)

Materials

For three cushions, 1/2 yd. (45 cm) of linen 62-1/2 in. (160 cm) wide with 26 threads per inch (2.5 cm); pieces of blue-, red-, and green-plaid cotton (the size differs for various cushions); DMC or Anchor embroidery floss as indicated on the key to the chart plus brown #611 or #898; ecru sewing thread; 4-1/2 yds. (4 m) of ecru seam binding 1 in. (2.5 cm) wide; three pillow forms.

Directions

For the front, cut the linen as follows: for a pillow with five embroidered squares, cut five squares 4-3/4 x 4-3/4 in. (12 x 12 cm); for a pillow with a large embroidered square, cut one square 9-1/4 x 9-1/4 in. (24 x 24 cm); for the pillow with the house, cut one square 5-1/2 x 5-1/2 in. (14 x 14 cm) and four rectangles 2 x 5-1/2 in. (5 x 14 cm).

Cross-stitch the motif according to the chart, using three strands of floss over three threads. Outline stitch over completed cross-stitch, using three strands of brown #611 or #898 for the rocking chair and baskets. Zigzag machine stitch around the edges of each piece.

Cut the plaid fabric for the front as follows: for a pillow with five embroidered squares, cut four squares 4-3/4 x 4-3/4 in. (12 x 12 cm); for a pillow with a large embroidered square, cut four rectangles 3 x 9-1/4 in. (8 x 24 cm) and four squares 3 x 3 in. (8 x 8 cm); for the pillow with the house, cut four rectangles 3 in. x 5-1/2 in. (8 x 14 cm), four squares 3 x 3 in. (8 x 8 cm), four squares 2 x 2 in. (5 x 5 cm), and eight rectangles 2 x 3 in. (5 x 8 cm).

Sew the patchwork pieces for the front of the cushion together, using the photo as a guide, with 1/4 in. (1 cm) seam allowances.

For the back of each pillow, cut two rectangles of plaid fabric 10-1/2 x 13-1/2 in. (27 x 35 cm). Make a hem 1 in. (2.5 cm) wide with a 1/4 in. (1 cm) inner hem along one long side of each back piece. Overlap the hemmed edges and tack in place so that the back is the same size as the front. With right sides together, sew around the edges of the back and front. Turn right side out. Insert the pillow form.

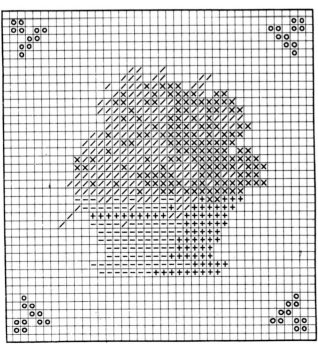

Key to Charts

DMC Anchor

House

·	= ecru	ecru	387
●	= medium dark delft	322	978
X	= salmon	352	9
╱	= medium jade	368	214
—	= cobalt	3325	129

Baskets

○	= wine	224	893
+	= salmon	352	9
X	= juniper	367	217
╱	= medium jade	368	214
—	= light cocoa	754	1012

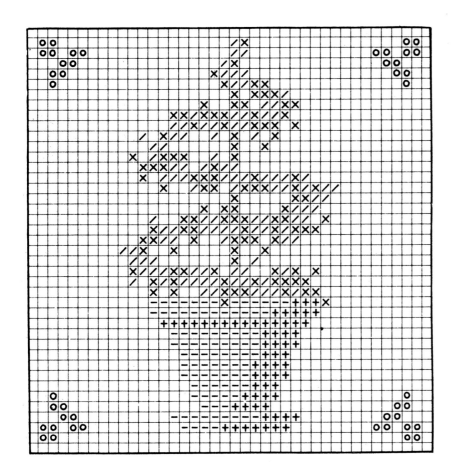

Key to Charts

		DMC	Anchor
Potted Plant			
○	= wine	224	893
+	= salmon	352	9
X	= juniper	367	217
/	= medium jade	368	214
−	= light cocoa	754	1012
Hearts			
·	= ecru	ecru	387
○	= medium wine	223	895
/	= wine	224	893
●	= medium dark delft	322	978
X	= salmon	352	9
\	= medium jade	368	214
ǀ	= light cocoa	754	1012
−	= cobalt	3325	129

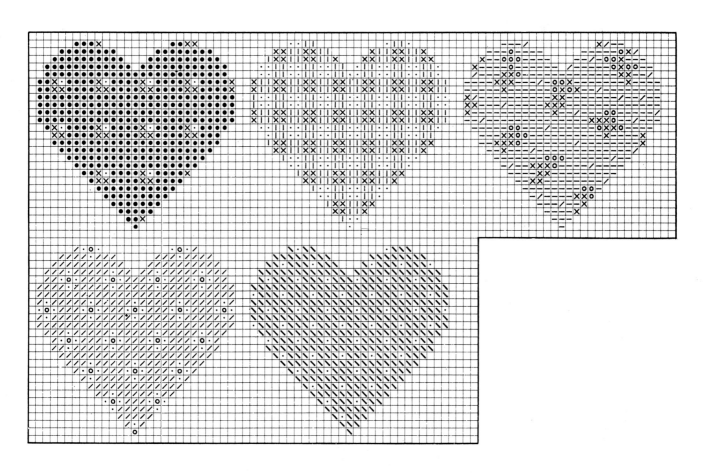

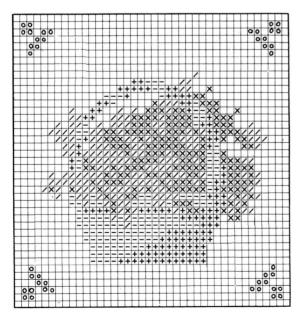

Key to Charts

		DMC	Anchor
Tree			
●	= medium dark delft	322	978
╱	= salmon	352	9
X	= medium jade	368	214
I	= tan	738	362
+	= cobalt	3325	129
Basket			
○	= wine	224	893
+	= salmon	352	9
X	= juniper	367	217
╱	= medium jade	368	21
−	= light cocoa	754	1012

Key to Charts

DMC Anchor

Wreath

		DMC	Anchor
◺	= salmon	352	9
●	= juniper	367	217
▬	= medium jade	368	214
✚	= dark chartreuse	471	255
·	= light cocoa	754	1012
✕	= medium coral	3328	1024
◿	= avocado	3346	267

Topiary

		DMC	Anchor
○	= wine	224	893
✚	= salmon	352	9
✕	= juniper	367	217
◿	= medium jade	368	214
▬	= light cocoa	754	1012

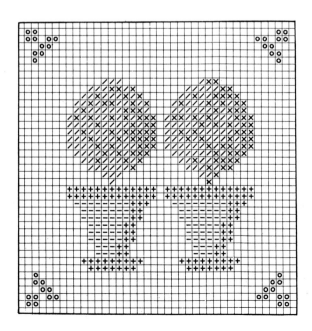

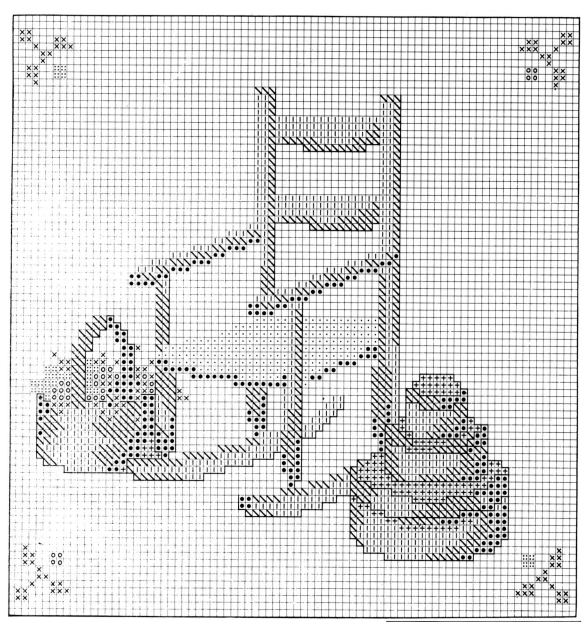

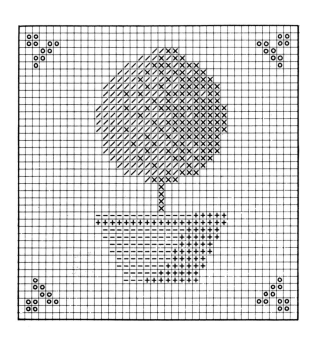

Key to Charts

	DMC	Anchor
Rocker		
○ = medium wine	223	895
⦂ = salmon	352	9
X = medium jade	368	214
◺ = nutmeg	420	374
● = brown	434	370
+ = dark tan	435	365
I = tan	738	362
· = light sand	739	885
Topiary		
○ = wine	224	893
+ = salmon	352	9
X = juniper	367	217
◺ = medium jade	368	214
— = light cocoa	754	1012

Tunisian Rug

This contemporary mosaic rug complements all kinds of looks—western or southwestern, tropical, Oriental, traditional. Once you've created such a work of art, though, could you actually let anyone walk on it?

Finished Measurements
49 x 63-1/2 in. (126 x 163 cm)

Materials

2 yd. (1.82 m) of rug canvas 58-1/2 in. (150 cm) wide with 13 squares per 4 in. (10 cm); Anchor rug wool, or its equivalent, as indicated on the key to the chart; 6-2/3 yd. (6 m) of seam binding 1-1/2 in. (4 cm) wide; masking tape (optional).

Directions

Tape or machine baste around the edge of the canvas to keep it from raveling. With a magic marker, sketch in the positions of the motifs. Using one strand of wool over one double-thread crossing, cross-stitch the motifs according to the chart, beginning 2 in. (5 cm) from the lower right edge of the canvas. Trim the finished rug, leaving 1-1/4 in. (3.5 cm) of fabric beyond the embroidery all the way around. Sew seam binding along the edges, fold the edges under, and sew them to the back.

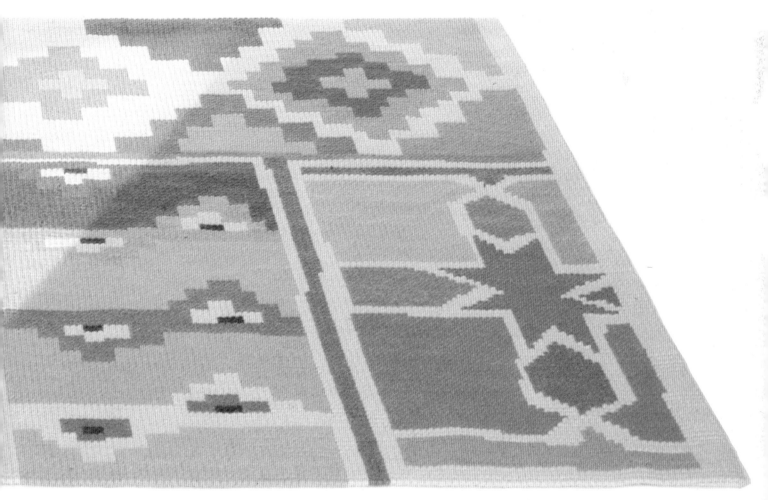

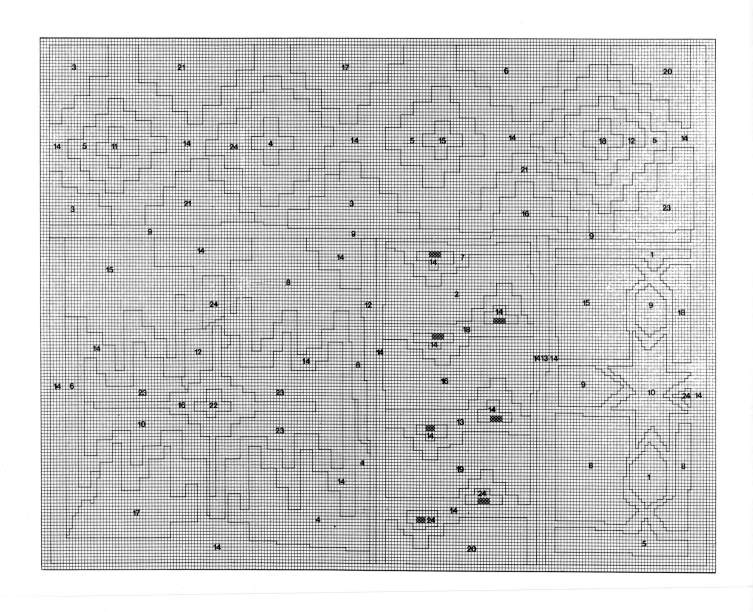

Key to Chart

Anchor Rug Wool		Anchor Rug Wool		Anchor Rug Wool	
1 = ocher	3013	9 = salmon	3163	17 = dark yellow	3230
2 = brown	3045	10 = green	3174	18 = light blue	3257
3 = light brown	3064	11 = tan	3178	19 = beige	3276
4 = gray blue	3077	12 = orange	3183	20 = light pink	3290
5 = soft green	3086	13 = soft brown	3192	21 = gray	3440
6 = moss green	3100	14 = ecru	3204	x and 22 = dark gray	3442
7 = blue green	3140	15 = light lilac	3225	23 = pink	3893
8 = blue	3145	16 = yellow	3229	24 = dark pink	3894

Santa Egg Warmer

Although designed as egg warmers, these Santas can double as Christmas-tree ornaments or table decorations. For place cards or gifts, initials stitched onto the gift Santa's holding behind his back would add a special finishing touch.

Finished Measurements
4-3/4 x 6 in. (12 x 15 cm)

Materials
Ecru Aida cloth 14 x 8 in. (36 x 21 cm) with 8 threads per inch (2.5 cm); DMC or Anchor embroidery floss as indicated on the key to the chart; for the lining, red cotton 7-3/4 x 11-3/4 in. (20 x 30 cm), fiberfill stuffing, red sewing thread, a bell with a diameter of 1/2 in. (1.5 cm).

Directions
Beginning at the lower right edge, 1-1/2 in. (4 cm) from the edge, cross-stitch the Aida cloth for the front and back of Santa according to the chart, leaving a space of 1 in. (2.5 cm) between the two figures. Work each cross-stitch using all six strands of embroidery floss over one thread group. Outline in stem stitch over completed cross-stitch, using two strands of black floss, around the beard and hairline, the eyebrows and moustache, the belt buckle and cuffs.

Cut out the embroidered Santas, allowing 1/2 in. (1.5 cm) for a seam. Cut out two pieces of red cotton the same size as the Santas, for the lining. Place the two embroidered pieces right sides together and sew along their outside edges, leaving the lower edge open. Zigzag stitch around all the edges. Turn the Santa right side out and line it with a small amount of fiberfill. Place the red cotton pieces right sides together and sew around their edges, leaving the lower edge open. Insert the cotton in the Santa, arranging the fiberfill evenly between the lining and the Aida cloth. Fold hems to the inside and slip stitch them in place. Sew the bell on top.

Key to Chart

		DMC	Anchor
·	= white	white	1
●	= black	310	403
◥	= blossom pink	326	59
∴	= light gray	415	398
)	= light rosebud pink	604	55
✕	= light red	666	46
△	= bottle green	702	226
◡	= very light ecru	712	926
⊔	= pink	776	24
∴	= med. blossom pink	899	52
⊔	= copper	945	881
◡	= medium jonquil	973	297

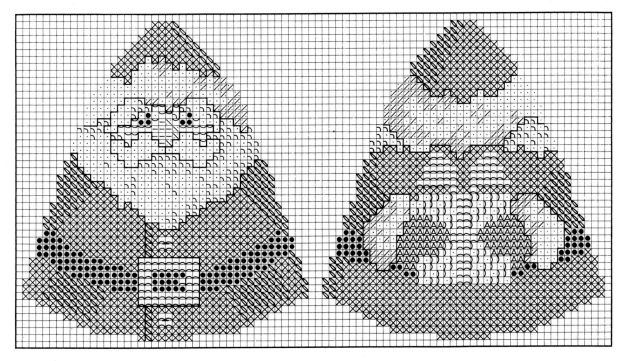

Cherub Napkins

A whole band of chubby cherubim, one at each place,

or a special Christmas cherub on a bread cloth—a cheerful note

for a holiday table, either way.

Finished Measurements
13-1/2 x 13-1/2 in. (35 x 35 cm)

Materials

For six napkins, 1 yd. (.9 m) of linen 62-1/2 in. (160 cm) wide with 26 threads per inch (2.5 cm); DMC or Anchor embroidery floss as indicated on the key to the chart.

Directions

For each napkin, cut a piece of linen 17-1/2 x 17-1/2 in. (45 x 45 cm), being careful to keep threads straight. Make a hem 1 in. (2.5 cm) wide with an inner hem and miter the corners (see the basic instructions). In the lower right corner, cross-stitch the cherub, using two strands of floss over two threads. Begin with the wings, 1 in. (2.5 cm) from the right edge and 2 in. (5.5 cm) from the lower edge.

Outline stitch over completed cross-stitch, using one strand of embroidery floss, above the eyes in tan, by the ears in light sand, and around all the remaining stitches in light brick.

Key to Chart			
		DMC	**Anchor**
‖	= salmon	352	9
O	= light salmon	353	6
=	= tan	437	362
V	= camel	676	891
·	= very light ecru	712	926
◉	= dark salmon	817	13
+	= medium light beige	950	376
I	= light copper	951	880
●	= light rust	977	363
⊠	= light sand	3045	888
T	= light antique blue	3753	1031
−	= very light delft	3756	1037
·	= light beige	3774	778
H	= light brick	3778	1013

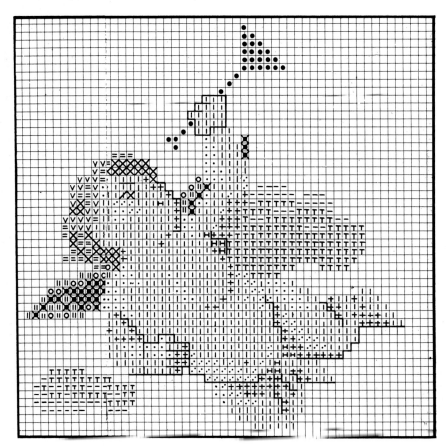

FOR KIDS ONLY

Jungle Sampler and Towel

Even the letters have spots in this jumping jungle sampler, whose grinning monkeys have swung clear out of the frame and landed on a matching towel almost guaranteed to lure reluctant kids into the tub.

Sampler Finished Measurements
19 x 23-1/2 in (49 x 60 cm)

27½"x22½"

Materials *14 HOLES. INCH*

For the sampler, 27-1/4 x 31-1/4 in. (70 x 80 cm) of white cotton embroidery fabric with 25 threads per inch (2.5 cm) and a matching frame; for the towel, a purchased towel, linen the width of the towel with 20 threads per inch (2.5 cm), and basting thread; for both sampler and towel, DMC or Anchor embroidery floss as indicated on the key to the chart.

Directions
Sampler

Cross-stitch the motif according to the chart, using two strands of floss over two threads. Begin 5-1/4 in. (13.5 cm) from the right side and lower edge. Embroider dots in satin stitch and eyes in French knots with one strand of black floss.

Outline stitch over completed cross-stitch, using one strand of floss: outline the giraffe on the upper right with terra cotta; the coconut with brown; the remaining giraffes with brick; the two large lions with medium rust; the small lion with dark rust; the pair of tigers and the small tiger at the bottom with medium apricot; the middle elephant at the bottom and the leopard with dark gray; the rhinos and the remaining elephants with dark fog; the lone sitting tigers, the zebras, both butterflies (two strands), and all whiskers and mouths with black; the leaves with parrot green; and the remaining figures in a matching color or one shade darker.

With the photo as a guide, embroider the name in the open space between the butterflies, using letters from the sampler alphabet. (See the basic instructions for spacing hints.) Frame the finished picture.

Towel

Baste the linen to the towel where you want the motif. Cross-stitch one of the swinging monkey motifs from the sampler, using three strands of floss over two threads of linen and stitching through both the linen and the towel. Outline stitch over completed cross-stitch, using two strands of floss. For the mouth and eyes, use three strands of floss in a French knot stitch. Remove basting and trim excess linen close to stitching.

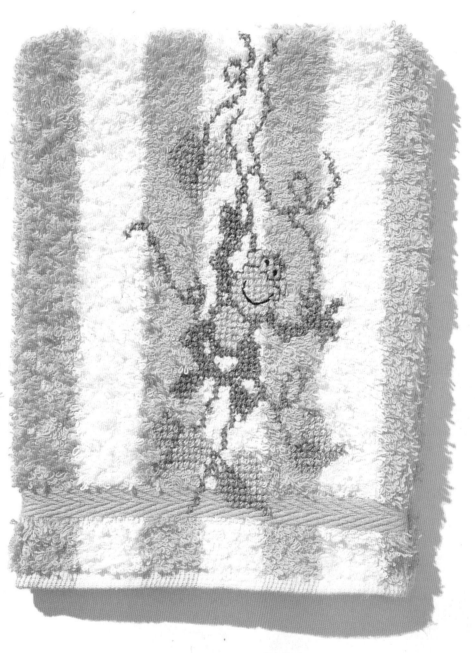

Key to Chart

		DMC	Anchor
·	= white	white	2
●	= cinnamon	301	1049
■	= black	310	403
◩	= light red	349	46
✳	= brick	356	5975
◻	= light cinnamon	402	1047
◻	= dark gray	414	235
◻	= light gray	415	398
⊞	= light toast	436	1045
◻	= dark fog	451	233
◻	= light fog	453	231
◻	= light chartreuse	472	253
◻	= med. spring green	703	238
◻	= medium apricot	721	324
◻	= light orange	743	302
◻	= medium peach	744	301
·	= peach	745	300
◻	= light peach	746	386
◻	= light loden green	772	259
▲	= dark cobalt	798	131
+	= medium cobalt	809	130
◣	= dark fawn	840	379
◻	= parrot green	905	257
◸	= dark chartreuse	907	255
◻	= dark mint green	911	205
⊠	= terra cotta	921	338
◻	= dark rust	922	1003
◻	= copper	945	881
◻	= medium rust	976	1001
◻	= light rust	977	1002

Snow Bunny Curtains and Quilt

*An imaginative young mind is sure to build stories around the
lively snow bunnies on these colorful curtains and quilt—
beginning, perhaps, with the Bunny Winter Olympics?*

Curtain Finished Measurements
20 x 35-1/2 (51 x 91 cm)

Quilt Finished Measurements
33-1/2 x 33-1/2 in. (86 x 86 cm)

Curtains

Materials

Purchased curtains or blue-dotted fabric 18 x 36 in. (46 x 92.5 cm) and white cotton 20-3/4 x 36 in. (53 x 92.5 cm) for the backing; white Hardanger cloth 6 x 36 in. (15 x 92.5 cm) with 23 double threads per inch (2.5 cm); DMC or Anchor embroidery floss as indicated on the key to the chart; curtain rings.

Directions

In whatever pattern pleases you, cross-stitch the snow bunnies on the Hardanger cloth according to the chart an inch from the edge of the fabric, using two threads of floss over two double threads. (On purchased curtains, you can either sew the Hardanger to the curtain first and embroider through both thicknesses, or embroider on the Hardanger, then sew the embroidered piece to the curtains.) Outline stitch over completed cross-stitch according to the chart, using one strand of black floss.

To make the curtains from scratch, cut a piece of dotted fabric 11-1/2 x 36 in. (29.5 x 92.5 cm) and a piece 4-3/4 x 36 in. (12 x 92.5 cm). Cut the Hardanger fabric with a 1/4 in. (1 cm) seam allowance. Sew the large piece of fabric to the upper edge of the Hardanger cloth and the small piece to the lower edge. Press the seam away from the Hardanger cloth and topstitch 1/4 in. (1 cm) from the edge of the embroidered insert. Place the dotted fabric and the white cotton right sides together and sew around the edges, leaving an opening on one side. Turn right side out and sew the opening closed. Press around the edges. For a sharper edge, topstitch all the way around.

Key to Chart

		DMC	Anchor
·	= white	white	2
■	= black	310	403
⠿	= gray	318	399
◺	= brown	434	370
⊏	= light toast	436	1045
◺	= blossom pink	605	50
╱	= light red	666	46
⋁	= bottle green	702	226
○	= light parrot green	704	256
╟	= tan	738	362
●	= light navy	797	132
⊠	= dark cobalt	798	131
⌞	= medium cobalt	809	130
◺	= medium jonquil	973	297

Note: To topstitch, hand or machine sew a line of small, closely spaced running stitches on the right side of the fabric near the seam.

For both purchased and hand-sewn curtains, sew or attach curtain rings.

Quilt

Materials

For the patchwork squares, 18 in. (46 cm) of white-on-pink dotted fabric and 18 in. (46 cm) of white-on-blue dotted fabric; for the border and back, 6 in. (15 cm) of pink-on-white dotted fabric and 45 in. (1.2 m) of blue-on-white dotted fabric, all 35 in. (90 cm) wide; white Aida cloth 6 x 48 in. (15 x 123 cm) with 14 double threads per inch (2.5 cm); DMC or Anchor embroidery floss as indicated on the key to the chart; white sewing thread.

Directions

Cut eight squares 6 x 6 in. (15 x 15 cm) from the Aida cloth. Using two strands of embroidery floss over one thread group, cross-stitch one bunny motif in the center of each square, according to the chart. Outline stitch over completed cross-stitch, using one strand of black floss. Trim the squares to 4-3/4 x 4-3/4 in. (12 x 12 cm).

Cut twenty-two squares of white-on-pink dotted fabric and nineteen squares of white-on-blue dotted fabric 4-3/4 x 4-3/4 in. (12 x 12 cm) square. Cut two strips 2-3/4 in. x 35 in. (7 x 90 cm) of the pink-on-white dotted fabric. From the blue-on-white dotted fabric, cut two strips 2-3/4 x 35 in. (7 x 90 cm) and a piece 35 x 35 in. (90 x 90 cm) for the back.

The finished blanket will be seven squares in length and width. Sew the squares together according to the diagram. Use a 1/4 in. (1 cm) seam allowance.

Sew the pink-on-white dotted fabric strips along the top and bottom edges and the blue-on-white dotted fabric at the sides, making mitered corners (see the basic instructions). Pin the back and front pieces right sides together and sew around three sides, making a 1/2 in. (1.5 cm) seam. Turn right side out and sew the fourth side.

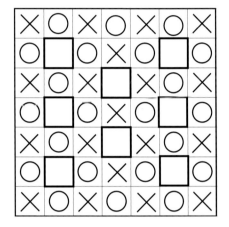

X = WHITE-ON-BLUE SQUARE
O = WHITE-ON-PINK SQUARE
☐ = EMBROIDERED SQUARE

Nautical Sampler

*Sailors, skin divers, seals, sailboats, starfish, shells—even the
sounds of the sea words in this sampler echo the murmur of surf.
Sure to tug like the tide at a young imagination, it makes a delightful
introduction to nautical wonders for the sailor-to-be.*

Nautical Sampler

Finished Measurements
21-3/4 x 25-3/4 in. (56 x 66 cm)
Embroidery Measurements
19 x 23 in. (49 x 59 cm)

Materials

31-1/4 x 35 in. (80 x 90 cm) of white Aida cloth with 11-1/2 thread groups per inch (2.5 cm); DMC or Anchor embroidery floss as indicated on the key to the chart; white and red cotton yarn; a matching frame.

Directions

Beginning with the lower right-hand corner of the design 6-1/4 in. (16 cm) from the side and lower edge of the Aida cloth, cross-stitch according to the chart, using three strands of floss over one thread group. In the open space, embroider the name and birth date. (See the basic instructions for spacing hints.)

Stem stitch over completed cross-stitch, using two strands of floss: outline the windows of the blue lighthouse, the shells and starfish, and the gray section of the light house at the lower right with red; outline the windows of the red light buoys with light emerald; outline the children's faces and bodies and the strips of the light with dark melon; work all remaining outline stitches in black. Using three strands of black floss, make tiny stitches for the mast lines on the boats in the second row from the bottom and make French knots for eyes (see the photo).

Embroider the border in slanted satin stitch using one strand of cotton yarn over two thread groups. Alternate three stitches of red with two stitches of white. Frame the finished picture.

Key to Chart

		DMC	Anchor
·	= white	white	2
◢	= black (2 strands)	310	403
◿	= light charcoal	317	400
◺	= gray	318	399
▲	= dark cherry	498	1005
◹	= medium magenta	603	62
◿	= med. light pewter	647	1040
◺	= light pewter	648	900
◹	= light red (2 strands)	666	46
✳	= light emerald	700	228
◿	= bottle green	702	226
∷	= light parrot green	704	256
⊥	= light camel	729	890
◺	= dark orange	741	304
◹	= orange	742	303
▭	= light cobalt	775	128
●	= navy	796	133
⊠	= dark cobalt (3 strands)	798	131
◿	= light bluebird blue	799	136
◖	= light indigo	800	144
◹	= medium seafoam (2 strands)	928	274
⊡	= dark antique blue	932	1033
◺	= dark melon (2 strands)	947	330
⊡	= light copper	951	880
◺	= light blush	963	73
▽	= medium jonquil	973	297
◡	= medium light sand	3046	887

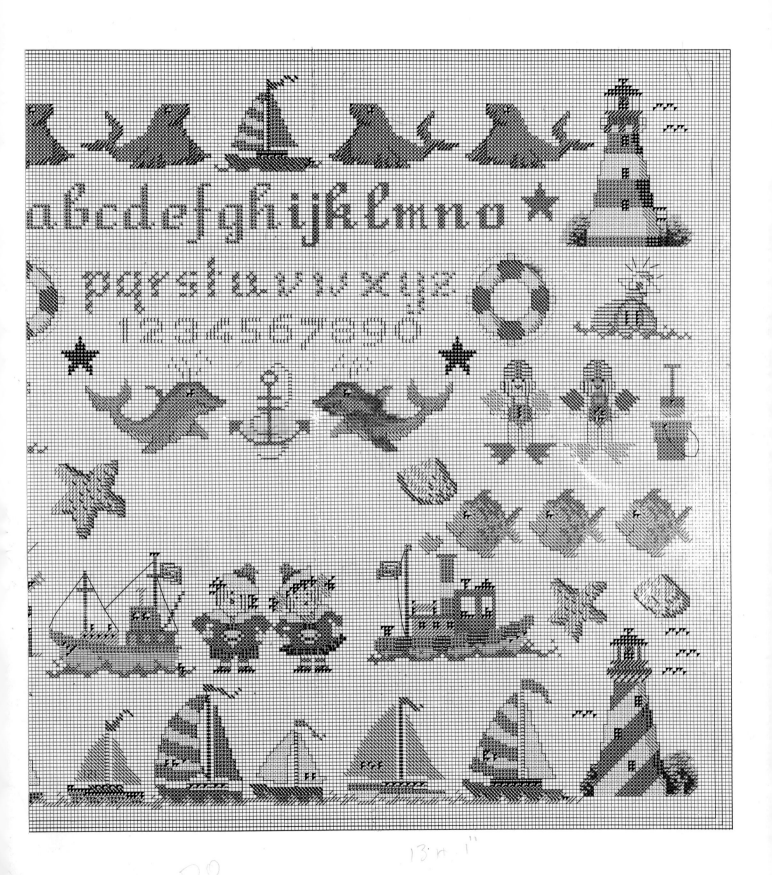

Nautical Book Cover

A book cover for a photo album, a baby book, a journal,

a daily log—any figure from the nautical sampler would work here,

as a matching project or on its own.

Finished Measurements
5-1/2 x 7 in. (14 x 18 cm)

Materials

Purchased book; a piece of white Aida cloth with 17 thread groups per inch (2.5 cm) large enough to wrap around the book, allowing for a 3/4 in. (2 cm) seam all the way around; a piece of white flannel the same size; DMC or Anchor embroidery floss as indicated on the key to the chart plus orange #742 or #303; enough red-and-white striped seam binding to bind all the edges.

Directions

Place the book on the wrong side of the Aida cloth and mark the spine and edges of the book on the cloth with pins or light pencil. Center and cross-stitch the diver (or any figure you choose) from the sampler, using three strands of floss over two thread groups. Outline stitch over completed cross-stitch as for the sampler. For the diver in this project, use two strands of black floss around the hat and in a French knot for the eyes, three strands of light red floss for the mouth, and the remaining outline stitches in orange #742 or #303.

Embroider the name and date from the sampler under the diver, if you wish, flanked by a pail and shovel from the sampler (see the photo). Work each cross-stitch using two strands of floss over one thread group and outline stitch over completed cross-stitch using one strand of black floss.

Cut the flannel in half and turn under a 1 in. (2.5 cm) hem on one side of each piece. Place the flannel on the embroidered cloth, wrong sides together, with raw edges lined up. (The two hemmed edges of the backing should be about 2 in. (5 cm) apart in the center.) Baste the flannel to the embroidered cloth. Sew seam binding around the outside, covering the raw edges. Insert the book through the opening in the flannel backing.

Backpack

It's a happy backpacker who totes a personalized backpack.

Changing the name on the chart is a cinch,

and with a little artistry the soccer ball can become a sketch pad,

a football, a skateboard, a camera…

Embroidery Measurements
2 x 2-3/4 in. (5 x 7 cm)

Materials

4 x 4 in. (10 x 10 cm) of linen with 25 threads per inch (2.5 cm) or equivalent needlepoint canvas (see note); DMC or Anchor embroidery floss as indicated on the key to the chart; a purchased backpack.

Note: You may choose to use needlepoint canvas to make a

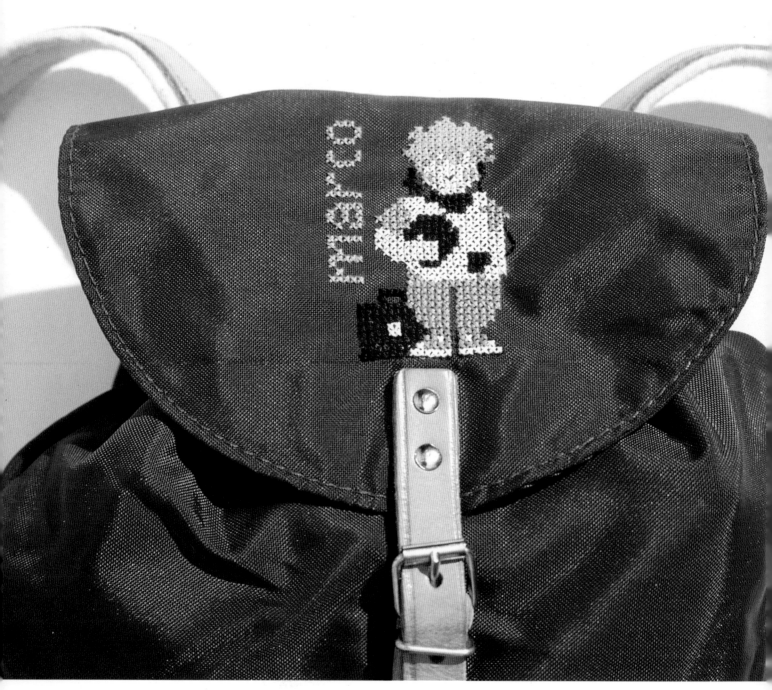

removeable grid, rather than
linen. See page 11.

Directions

Baste the linen to the desired
spot on the backpack. Working
through both thicknesses, cross-
stitch the motif according to the
chart, using two strands of floss
over two threads. Outline stitch
over completed cross-stitch,
using two strands of floss: outline the gym shoes in light red
and the rest in black. Embroider
the backpacker's name to the
left of the child. Trim the excess
linen close to your embroidery.

Key to Chart		
	DMC	**Anchor**
⊡ = white	white	2
◪ = yellow	307	289
◣ = black	310	403
⊠ = light red	666	46
● = medium spring green	703	238
◺ = light sand	739	885
◿ = dark orange	741	304
◹ = blossom pink	957	50
▲ = peacock blue	996	433

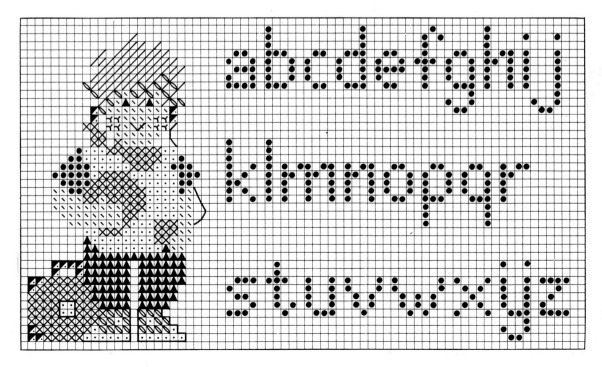

Toys Rug

The more toys on this rug, the better—what could be more child friendly? Varying colors or toys to reflect a child's favorites would give it that "Mine!" flavor dear to small hearts.

Finished Measurements
28 x 38 in. (70 x 96 cm)

Materials

Rug canvas 33 x 43 in. (84 x 110 cm) with 18 squares to 4 in. (10 cm); Mayflower Helarsgarn or equivalent worsted-weight cotton that is 86 yds. (78.6 m) in 1-3/4 oz. (50 g) as indicated on the key to the chart; 4 yd. (3.5 m) of seam binding 1-1/2 in. (4 cm) wide; masking tape (optional).

Directions

Tape or machine baste around the edge of the canvas to prevent raveling. Cross-stitch according to the chart, using one strand of cotton over one square. Begin at the lower right corner 2-3/4 in. (7 cm) from the edge. Fill in the background in ecru. Trim the canvas 1 in. (3 cm) from the edge of the embroidery and fold to the back. Sew seam binding around the edges.

Key to Chart

		Mayflower
☐	= ecru	901
❘	= yellow	909
⊠	= red	910
⬓	= blue	963
●	= brown	969

Train Sheet

Remember Robert Louis Stevenson's poem about
the Land of Counterpane, where a child's bed covers
become a landscape of hills and valleys?
Well, here's a train to get there—last stop the Land of Nod.

Embroidery Measurements
1-3/4 in. (4.5 cm) wide

Materials
White petite Aida band with red
border 1-3/4 in. (4.5 cm) wide
with 16-1/2 thread groups per
inch (2.5 cm); DMC or Anchor
embroidery floss as indicated on
the key to the chart; a purchased
sheet.

Directions
Cross-stitch the motif according
to the chart, using two strands of
floss over one thread group.
Repeat the motif the width of
the sheet. For the rail, begin two
thread groups from the edge.
Sew the embroidered border to
the top of the sheet, 1-3/4 in.
(4.5 cm) from the edge.

Key to Chart		DMC	Anchor
= yellow		307	289
= light red		666	46
= light navy		797	132
= light turquoise		993	185
= peacock blue		996	433

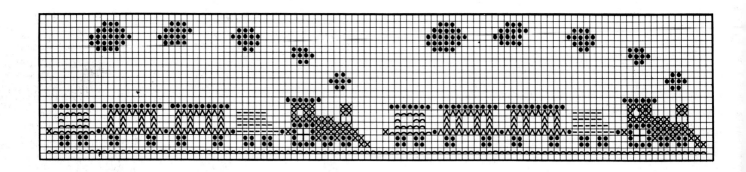

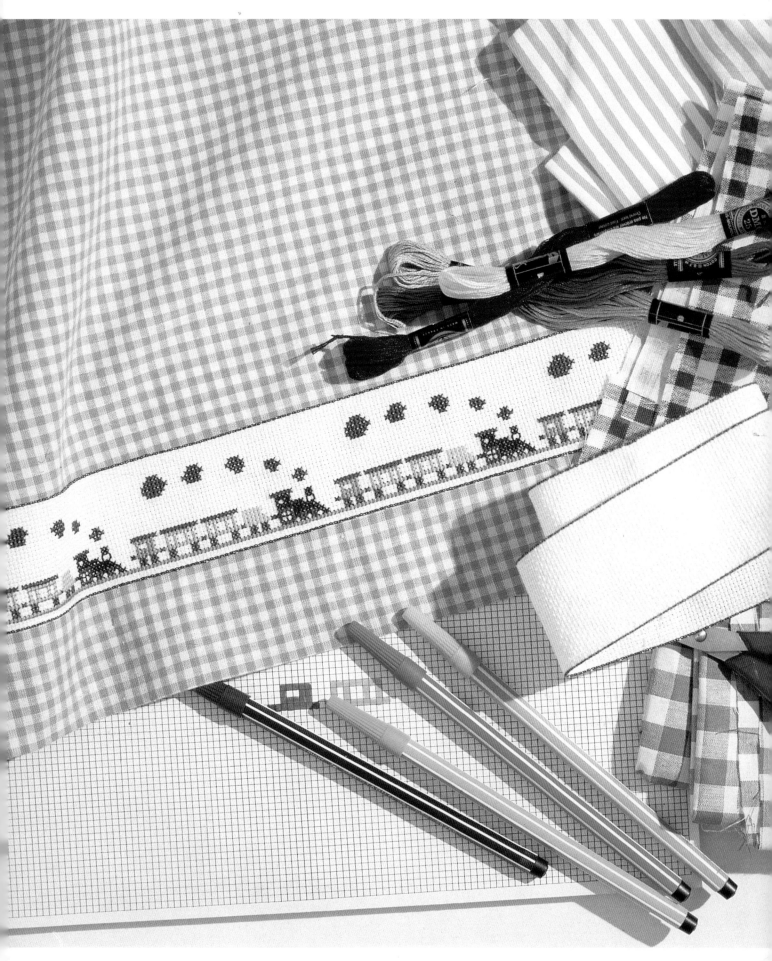

Kid Badges

For the small cowpoke or lion tamer, these badges transform the ordinary—T-shirt, sweatshirt, shorts, jeans, backpack—into the exciting.

Embroidery Measurements
3 x 4 in. (8 x 10 cm)

Materials

For each badge, 6 x 6 in. (15 x 15 cm) of white Hardanger fabric with 23 double threads per inch (2.5 cm) or Aida cloth with 14 thread groups per inch (2.5 cm); DMC or Anchor embroidery floss as indicated on the key to the charts; white sewing thread; a purchased T-shirt, sweatshirt, or other item you choose.

Note: The graph-paper design in the photo shows how you might create your own badges with different motifs.

Directions

Cross-stitch the motif according to the chart, beginning the outline square 3/4 in. (2 cm) from the edge. Use three strands of floss over two double threads or one thread group. For the jungle badge, stem stitch over completed cross-stitch, using three strands of black floss for the nose. Stem stitch the whiskers using one strand of black floss.

For both badges, trim the fabric 1/4 in. (1 cm) outside the embroidered areas. Fold the seam allowances under and sew the badge to the shirt or backpack. For a finishing touch, outline the upper and lower edges of the badge in cross-stitch on the shirt or backpack fabric, using three strands of floss in a contrasting color. Make each of these cross-stitches 1/4 in. (1 cm) wide with 1/4 in. (1 cm) between them.

Kid Badges

Key to Charts

		DMC	Anchor
Jungle Badge			
◣ = black		310	403
◹ = light rosebud pink		604	55
◺ = red orange		606	334
⊠ = med. spring green		703	238
◣ = dark cobalt		798	131
⊡ = terra cotta		921	338
◺ = medium jonquil		973	297
● = peacock blue		996	433
Cowboy Badge			
◣ = black		310	403
◺ = light azure		519	1038
◹ = light rosebud pink		604	55
◺ = red orange		606	334
⊠ = med. spring green		703	238
· = light orange		743	302
◣ = dark cobalt		798	131
● = emerald		910	229
◹ = terra cotta		921	338
◠ = light turquoise		993	185

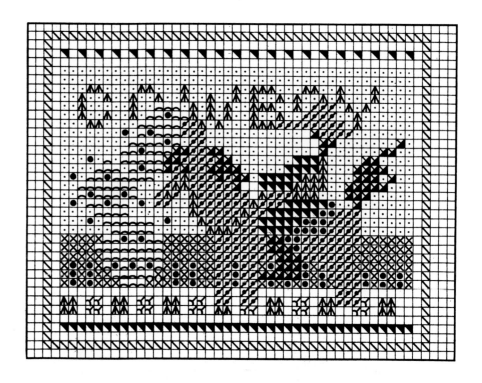

Bear Mittens and Scarf

For combatting the cold in high style, how dapper can you get for someone who can't even walk yet? Of course, the ensemble can be adapted for older brothers and sisters.

Embroidery Measurements
2 x 2-1/4 in. (5 x 6 cm)

Materials

Purchased mittens; for the scarf, two pieces of sweatshirt material 7 in. (18 cm) wide and of the desired length; two pieces of linen 6 x 6 in. (15 x 15 cm) for the mittens and one piece for the scarf, with 20 threads per inch (2.5 cm); DMC or Anchor embroidery floss as indicated on the keys to the charts.

Directions
Mittens

Baste a piece of linen in the center of each mitten. Cross-stitch the bear motif on the center of the linen according to one of the mitten charts, using two strands of floss over two threads. Outline stitch over completed cross-stitch, using one strand of black floss. Trim the excess linen. Reverse the motif for the second mitten, using the other mitten chart.

Scarf

Baste a piece of linen in the center of one piece of sweatshirt fabric 1 in. (2.5 cm) from the lower edge. Cross-stitch the bear motif on the center of the linen according to the chart, using three strands of floss over two threads. Outline stitch over completed cross-stitch, using two strands of black floss. Trim the excess linen. Place the two pieces of fabric right sides together and sew around the edges, leaving one end open. Turn right side out and sew the opening closed.

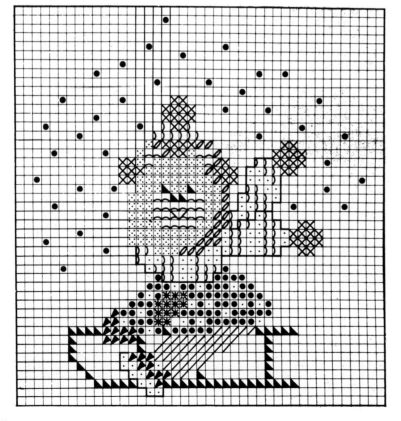

Key to Chart		DMC	Anchor
Scarf			
· = white		white	2
◣ = black		310	403
• = light gray		415	398
◹ = light toast		436	1045
⋮ = tan		738	362
◡ = light orange		743	302
◥ = dark cobalt		798	131
◿ = medium cobalt		809	130
✳ = dark cherry		3705	35
⊠ = light cherry		3706	33
◺ = very light cherry		3708	31

Key to Chart

DMC Anchor

Mittens

		DMC	Anchor
·	= white	white	2
◣	= black	310	403
●	= light gray	415	398
◿	= light toast	436	1045
◸	= azure	518	1039
◹	= light azure	519	1038
⦂	= tan	738	362
◠	= light orange	743	302
◣	= dark cobalt	798	131
∴	= medium cobalt	809	130
✳	= dark cherry	3705	35
⊠	= light cherry	3706	33
◡	= very light cherry	3708	31

Key to Chart

DMC Anchor

Mittens

		DMC	Anchor
·	= white	white	2
◣	= black	310	403
●	= light gray	415	398
◿	= light toast	436	1045
◸	= azure	518	1039
◹	= light azure	519	1038
⦂	= tan	738	362
◠	= light orange	743	302
◣	= dark cobalt	798	131
∴	= medium cobalt	809	130
✳	= dark cherry	3705	35
⊠	= light cherry	3706	33
◡	= very light cherry	3708	31

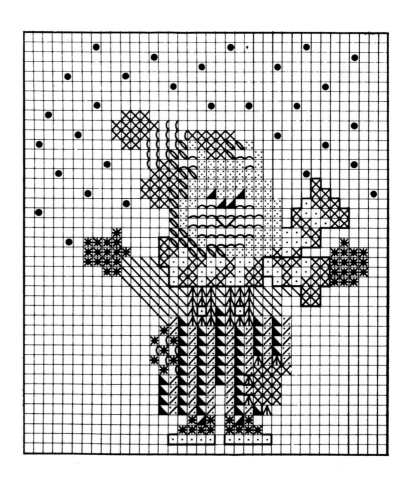

Bear Blanket

This blanket seems a likely candidate for adoption—
you know, that companion a child chooses to lug around
for months, if not years? It might be a good idea to make two.

Embroidery Measurements
13-1/2 x 14-3/4 in. (35 x 38 cm)

Materials

A white blanket; a piece of linen 15-1/2 x 17-1/2 in. (40 x 45 cm) with 13 threads per inch (2.5 cm); Anchor tapestry wool as indicated in the key to the chart plus light gray #497.

Directions

Baste the linen onto the center of the blanket. Cross-stitch the bear motif on the center of the linen according to the chart. Using one strand of wool over five threads, embroider through both thicknesses. Outline stitch over completed cross-stitch with light gray #497. Stem stitch the eyes and mouth with black. Trim the excess linen.

Key to Chart

Anchor Tapestry Wool

⊠	= pink	9
✳	= rose red	10
●	= dark blue	146
◡	= yellow	313
·	= white	402
◣	= black	403
∴	= blue	508
◿	= light blue	568
◿	= light pink	610
⠒	= light brown	702
⟋	= brown	742

Coverlet, Pillow, and Book

Surely a gift to cherish forever, this elegant threesome combines the beauty of tradition with a contemporary simplicity. With another color, different trim, create a Victorian look, a country effect...

Coverlet Finished Measurements
23-1/2 x 31-1/4 in. (60 x 80 cm)

Coverlet Embroidery Measurements
18-3/4 x 26 in. (48 x 67 cm)

Pillow Finished Measurements
11-3/4 x 15-1/2 in. (30 x 40 cm)

Coverlet

Materials

1 yd (.7 m) of white Aida cloth 50-3/4 in. (130 cm) wide with 11 thread groups per inch (2.5 cm); very light cherry embroidery floss (DMC #3708 or Anchor #31); 3-1/4 yd. (2.9 m) of white lace edging 1-1/2 in. (4 cm) wide with an openwork edge; 3-1/4 yd. (2.9 m) of pink ribbon to weave through the openwork edge; for the back, 1 yd. (.85 m) of white cotton 35 in. (90 cm) wide.

Directions

From the Aida cloth, cut a rectangle 27-1/4 x 34-1/4 in. (70 x 88 cm). Cross-stitch the motif according to the chart, using three strands of embroidery floss over one thread group. Begin with the outline in one of the lower corners, 3-1/2 in. (9 cm) from the side and the lower edge. When the embroidery is complete, trim the piece even on all edges, leaving 6 in. (15 cm) at the lower edge. Sew the lace ruffle 1/2 in. (1.5 cm) from the outside edges, gathering it at the corners to fit (see photo).

Place back and front right sides together and sew along three sides, rounding the corners at the upper edge, taking care not to catch the lace in the seam. Turn right side out. Baste or slip stitch the fourth side. Thread a ribbon through the openwork lace.

Pillow

Materials

15-1/2 x 22 in. (40 x 56.5 cm) of white cotton; 2 in. (5 cm) wide band of Aida cloth with a pink border, with 15 thread groups per inch (2.5 cm); very light cherry embroidery floss (DMC #3708 or Anchor #31); 1 yd. (.9 m) of white lace edging 1-1/2 in. (4 cm) wide with an openwork edge; 1 yd. (.9 m) of pink ribbon to weave through the openwork edge; cotton batting for filler.

Directions

Embroider the name with letters from the coverlet, using the top alphabet for the first letter and the lower alphabet for the rest. Center the name in the middle of the Aida band, two thread groups from the lower edge, and work each cross-stitch using four strands of floss over two thread groups. Frame the name with small hearts from the chart for the coverlet, six thread groups from the lower edge of the band; leave eight thread groups between the name and the hearts.

Make a paper pattern for the pillow slip based on the pattern pictured here. Cut two pieces of cotton from the pattern, allowing a 1/4 in. (1 cm) seam. Sew on the Aida cloth band 3-1/2 in. (9 cm) from the upper edge. On the right side of the front piece, pin the lace ruffle along the side and upper edges, with the bottom of the ruffle facing out. With front and back pieces right sides together and the lace in between, sew around the sides and upper edge. (Be sure not to catch the openwork of the lace in the seam.)

Turn the pillow slip right side out. Stuff it with batting and slip stitch the bottom closed. Thread the ribbon through the openwork lace.

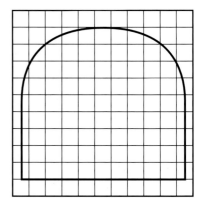

1 SQUARE = 1-1/2" (4 CM)

Annelies

A B C D E F
H I J K L M
N O P Q R S
T U V W X Y Z

A B C D E F H I J K L M
N O P R S T U X Y Z
a b c d e f g h i j k l m
n o p q r s t u v w x y z
1 2 3 4 5 6 7 8 9 0

Book Cover

Materials

A blank book or other book; a piece of pink-and-white Aida cloth with 25 threads per inch (2.5 cm) an inch (2.5 cm) wider than your book is tall and three and a half times longer than your book is wide; very light cherry embroidery floss (DMC #3708 or Anchor #31).

Directions

Decide where to place the motif on the Aida cloth by wrapping the cloth around your book and marking the edges of the front with pins or basting. Center the design within the marking and cross-stitch the appropriate initial from the large alphabet on the coverlet chart. Use three strands of embroidery floss over two thread groups.

Hem both ends of the cloth by turning under 1/2 in. (1.5 cm) and basting. Wrap the cloth around the book with the right side next to the book. With the book closed, make a book jacket by folding the ends of the fabric over the covers of the book. Pin the ends in place. Remove the book and slip stitch the sides of the pinned ends, making pockets for the book to fit into. Turn the fabric right side out. Fold the exposed raw edges under and slip stitch to the wrong side.

Special thanks to Betsy Frady of Calico Cross Stitch in Arden, North Carolina, for the items pictured on page 12, and to Dana Irwin for the loan of her grandmother's thimbles on page 8.

Index